EVOLVE   EMPOWER   ELEVATE

KRISTINA PERDUE

dedication

to anyone who dares to dream big and believe

and to bunny, of course

Acknowledgements

I need to acknowledge my husband for letting me take over the kitchen table with all my books, notes, files, pads of paper, Ticonderoga pencils, and their shavings, post-it notes, felt tip pens, highlighters, coffee cups, water bottles, Moroccan tea cups, and Good & Plenty candy boxes.

Oh, and thanks for making dinner again.

I also want to acknowledge all the authors, whose published works fed me the knowledge I thirsted for in my investigation. There are too many to list here and some of the works I read gave me great ammunition for the science element, but, oh my, *yawns*. However, I must acknowledge my favorites of which were Deepak Chopra, Brian Greene, Michael Singer, Joe Dispenza and Stephen Hawking.

I also feel called to recognize a sweet group of gals (we call ourselves the golden girls) who I chanced upon over three years ago in an online Marco Polo group for a 21 day alcohol free challenge we all signed up for. This was a turning point in my life to get serious about my personal growth and to this day, we still lean on and support each other although we live in different states across the country.

To my friends and family, if I didn't call or text you back in a timely manner, I apologize. Writing this book has completely consumed me, in a good way.

I'll call ya tomorrow. Hi Dad! *waves*

Contents

How I Manifested a Better Life Against All Odds

"The mind is like a parachute, it only works when it's open." - *Frank Zappa*

Heard all the talk about manifesting? I bet you have. The idea that you can manifest whatever you want has been all the rage lately. Just a quick search on Google or YouTube, or a scroll through TikTok or Instagram, and you'll be bombarded with posts about manifestation. You'll see these bold claims, like "you will be sent $5000 in the mail tomorrow" if you share or like a post. Or you'll get lucky numbers that are supposed to work like magic to bring you abundance. There are memes, GIFs, and quotes that sound promising. But honestly, sometimes it all seems a bit crazy, like something only a fool would buy into.

Let me address the skepticism you may have about manifestation. I understand why it can seem far-fetched or even outrageous. I mean, who wouldn't be skeptical of promises like receiving a large sum of money just by sharing a post? Yet, I knew there had to be more to it. That's exactly why I started diving deeper into the world of manifestation, reading and researching everything I could on the topic. If a title said "manifestation", I had to read it. I've gone through countless self-help books, works by all the popular gurus, blogs from life coaches, and of course all the celebrities and motivational speakers. I've explored spiritual books too, delving into the canon of almost every world religion.

And along the way, I stumbled upon some of the science behind it all, which fascinated me to no end. I have determined that manifestation is not some New Age mumbo jumbo for gullible knuckleheads.

To my surprise, I have discovered that there is a significant amount of scientific evidence supporting the reality of the art of manifesting. The problem for me was that one book might only report on one or two aspects of the science, and the next book might expound on an entirely different piece of scientific evidence altogether. As I researched and uncovered all this amazing proof from the scientific community, I realized no one so far has gathered together all of the compelling evidence that I had gleaned from a myriad of sources on the subject. This is one of the reasons I am writing this book!

When I first learned about quantum physics, my obsession took hold. I started devouring books by all the great scientists and physicists. I became engrossed in topics like the universe, astronomy, black holes, and the cosmos. And you know what? There exists an ever advancing interest of the scientific community about the ideas associated with manifestation and a good number of theoretical physicists who are conducting research studies on this topic right now. It's not just some frivolous idea. What I have attempted to do in this book, is to gather every spec of scientific knowledge related to this topic, so that it's all in one manuscript.

I want my readers to discover what I think is a very compelling amount of evidence relating to the art of manifestation.

Manifestation goes beyond superficial claims. There is a hidden art to it—an art that can be explained, understood and replicated. It's about tapping into the power of our thoughts, beliefs, and intentions to shape our reality. Quantum physics teaches us that at the most fundamental level, everything in the universe is made up of energy and vibrations. And our thoughts and emotions are also forms of energy, capable of influencing the world around us.

By understanding this connection between our thoughts and the universe, we can begin to harness the power of manifestation. It requires more than just wishful thinking or repeating affirmations. It's about aligning our thoughts, beliefs, and emotions with our desires, and then taking inspired action to bring them to fruition.

But here's the frustrating part: why has it been so difficult to find this information? I mean, I dug deep and schooled myself in books on science, biology, physiology, neuroscience, astronomy, the study of the cosmos, theoretical physics and quantum mechanics. It almost feels like a conspiracy, like someone has been deliberately hiding this crucial knowledge from the masses. I don't want to dwell on that now. Instead, I want to share with you what I have learned. You see, I am a teacher by profession, but I am also a seeker, always curious and eager to uncover the truth and it is in my nature to pass on knowledge.

A Little About Me

Let me share about myself for a moment. When I was a little girl, like maybe 3 or 4 years old, I remember that I was always dancing around my room and singing along to my favorite album, *Tina the Ballerina*. I would perform for anyone who would watch, hoping to be seen and appreciated for my talent. My ultimate desire was to be singing and dancing on stage. It was my dream to be a famous performer somehow. One day I found myself at an audition to be on television for a show called Romper Room (aging myself here). Obviously my parents had set this up somehow, but it's not like they had any connections to the entertainment industry. I don't really know how it happened, but for me, I felt like the luckiest little girl in the world. Just being there on set was a mind-blowing experience for me, an experience that impacted my outlook on life–that anything is possible and dreams can manifest into our reality.

At the age of 12, I had another opportunity to audition for a performance of the *Sound of Music* at a dinner theater. Unfortunately, my friend got the part and I didn't. However, this setback didn't stop me from dreaming about being on that stage. It was all I thought about! And one day, I received a call to audition again when a cast member left the show. This time, I got the part! It was a moment that made me believe that dreams can come true with perseverance and belief in oneself.

When I started high school, I was a shy and intimidated student. But deep down, I had a burning desire to make the Song Leading squad one day. I admired my friend's older sister, who was the captain of the varsity squad, and I kept a particular photo of her in my mind's eye. As a freshman, I kept that image close and imagined myself in her place. After making the junior varsity team my sophomore year, I continued to envision myself as the captain of the varsity team. And in my senior year, it happened. The visualization that played out over and over in my mind entered my reality. I was chosen as the captain, realizing that my heartfelt desires can come true with consistent dedication and faith.

Though these may seem like trivial accomplishments to some, at the time, they meant the world to me. Each of them took focus, time, and effort to manifest, but I never gave up. I wished, prayed, and hoped for my dreams to come true, and most importantly, I believed in myself. I took the necessary steps of action towards what I wanted, and each and every one of those desires eventually became a reality. I didn't know the term "manifestation" back then, but that's exactly what I was doing.

In all sincerity, I hope that through sharing my personal experiences and the knowledge I have gained, you can find inspiration and guidance on your own journey of manifesting. Whether you are new to the concept or have been intrigued by it for some time, I believe that by harnessing the power of manifestation, you can create positive changes in your life.

I recently did this. Two years ago I was a single mom, divorced and supporting two boys in college. I lived in my "crappy" apartment, drove my "crappy" car, and worked as a 5th grade teacher. I was unlucky in love, choosing the worst possible men to have relationships with and I felt stuck and powerless to change what had become of my life. But slowly, I started to put what I had been learning to the test.

One summer I decided to learn how to surf, both of my brothers were avid surfers and I figured I am pretty coordinated, I should be able to do it too. I spent money I didn't really have on a longboard and I drove at least 45 minutes to get to the beach, sometimes longer. I briefly dated a man who liked to surf and he took me down to San Clemente Beach a couple times to practice. Childhood memories flooded in as I realized this was where my family spent a couple summers camping at the beach.

I fell in love with that town all over again and decided that was where I wanted to live. I began to visualize my life there and of course it would be a life with everything else I wanted. After being single for six years I knew I didn't need a man to be happy, but I wanted a life partner. I meditated and did visualizations of how I would feel finding a man who loved me, who was kind, who was secure financially, who was passionate, who was active and up for life, who would ground me and challenge me and make me a better person. Someone my sons could embrace as a part of our family.

So guess what? It magically all came together! I purposefully manifested the love of my life, my best friend and soulmate, and we were recently married! I manifested a home near the beach and now when I rise from my pillow each morning the first thing I see is the ocean! I have enough money to support my boys as they embark on starting their own lives and we are closer and happier as a family than we've been in a long time. Writing this book is also part of my manifestation story. I have always wanted to be a published writer.

So, if you're willing to open your mind and explore the world of manifestation with me, I promise, you will be amazed at what you can achieve. Manifestation is not a quick fix or a magic trick, but a powerful tool that can transform your life from the inside out.

It is important to know that manifestation is not just about material things. It's about creating a life that is aligned with our true purpose and values—for the good of all and the harm of none. It is about living in abundance. It's about manifesting love, happiness, and success in all aspects of our lives and the lives of our family, friends, and loved ones. There is enough to go around for everyone! So let's set aside the skepticism and dive into the art and science of manifesting together. It's time to explore the power within ourselves and tap into the wonders of creation.

Let's embark on this journey together, discovering the true potential we have within ourselves, and embracing the limitless possibilities that await us. And through this journey, I believe you will learn some truly amazing things about yourself and the world we live in.

How do I use the Journal and Workbook Resources?

I suggest going out and purchasing a nice, new journal, and dedicating it to the activities and journal prompts in this book. This way you will have a record of what you are learning and how you are interpreting it. There are **JOURNAL AND WORKBOOK ACTIVITIES** at the end of most, but not all chapters. Some activities will ask you to copy down notes and many activities will find you recording personal reflections, taking inventory on your life and journaling in your journal daily.

I would encourage you to try to do every activity and answer every journal prompt, especially if these exercises are new to you. If you are further down the path in your personal growth, then do the activities that resonate with you. It can be very powerful to memorialize your thoughts and feelings in real time. And it is very insightful to go back to a journal and look at your growth and progress, examining where you were like, say a year from now.

The Universe Unveiled: Navigating Through the Matrix

"The intuitive mind is a sacred gift and the rational mind is a faithful servant. We have created a society that honors the servant and has forgotten the gift." - Albert Einstein

You must have seen or at least heard of the movie *The Matrix*. The movie's immense success catapulted the term *the matrix* into popular culture, eventually becoming synonymous with the idea that the physical world we live in is really a deceptive reality that shackles and restricts us.

But where did this term come from? The movie certainly popularized the term and played a significant role in shaping the collective consciousness, but it is not the actual origin. The concept of *the matrix* can be traced back to a rich tapestry of philosophical, scientific, and spiritual ideas that have evolved over centuries.

To truly understand the roots of the term, we must embark on a journey through time, exploring the works of great minds who laid the foundations for this captivating concept. One of the earliest philosophical musings can be found in the writings of Plato, the ancient Greek philosopher who introduced the allegory of the cave in his work *The Republic*.

In his allegory of the cave, Plato presents a scenario of individuals who have been imprisoned in a dark cave since birth, facing a blank wall with shadows projected onto it. These prisoners perceive the shadows as their reality, unaware of the greater truth beyond the cave. He uses the metaphor to suggest that our perception of the physical world may be limited, hinting at the idea of a deeper reality beyond our immediate senses.

Fast forward to the 17th century, where the famous philosopher René Descartes contemplated the nature of reality in his *Meditations on First Philosophy*. Descartes posed the notion that an all-powerful, deceiving entity could manipulate our senses, creating an illusory world. This idea, known as the *evil demon* hypothesis presents a cognitive dissonance between what we perceive and what actually exists.

The first to use the word *matrix* was mathematician James Joseph Sylvester in 1850. Sylvester defined a matrix to be an oblong arrangement of terms and saw it as something which led to various determinants from square arrays contained within it. In the movie, the humans were physically arranged as an array of batteries in pods resembling a womb to supply power to the machines. Matrix is related to the Latin word for "mother," originally meant "pregnant animal" or "breeding female" and was later generalized to mean "womb."

In the mid-20th century, renowned philosopher Jean Baudrillard introduced the idea of *the matrix* in his book *Simulacra and Simulation*, originally published almost twenty years before the release of the movie. Baudrillard argued that our modern society has become so saturated with images and simulations that we cannot distinguish between reality and fantasy. He describes a hyper-real simulation that shapes our perception of the world. Baudrillard's matrix is a web of illusions, a constructed reality from which we find it challenging to break free.

Moving into the 20th century, the term *the matrix* gained further prominence with the cyberpunk written works of authors like William Gibson. Gibson's influential novel *Neuromancer* explores a dystopian future where individuals are interconnected with a virtual world known as *the matrix*.

Today we find ourselves in the midst of a rapidly advancing technological revolution. This tide of innovation has given rise to the concept of virtual reality, a simulated electronic environment that can mimic or even surpass our physical reality in terms of sensory experience. It is this confluence of ancient philosophy and modern technology that birthed the full realization of the movie, *The Matrix*.

The Wachowski siblings, the creative geniuses behind the movie franchise, brilliantly fused together these philosophical, scientific, and literary ideas into a compelling and visually breathtaking narrative. They expanded upon the concept of *the matrix* to reflect a dystopian future and reimagined a world where humans are unknowingly trapped within a simulated reality created by sentient machines. This artificial construct aims to control and manipulate human perception, preventing individuals from discovering their true potential and the boundless possibilities that lie beyond their perceived world.

Therefore, while the movie *The Matrix* did not originate the term itself, it built upon centuries of philosophical and intellectual musings, presenting them in a visually stunning and thought-provoking manner that captivated audiences worldwide and led to the popularization of the term *the matrix* in contemporary culture.

This sparked countless discussions about the nature of reality, the limitations of perception, and the possibility of a deeper truth. Understanding the concept of *the matrix* empowers us to question the status quo, challenge our perceived realities, and break free from the limitations that society imposes.

Another popular phrase I hear a lot lately is *a glitch in the matrix*. What do we mean by a glitch in the matrix? It shouldn't be difficult to imagine that this expansive construct of the physical world we live in, is not without its flaws. Just as with any complex system, errors or glitches can occur. These glitches are the aberrations, the anomalies that defy the regular patterns and rules of our world. They are the moments when the facade cracks, revealing glimpses of an underlying truth, of a reality beyond the simulated realm, if you dare to believe that might be exactly what's going on in our world today.

A glitch in the matrix can take many forms and vary in intensity. It could be a minor hiccup, a fleeting feeling of déjà vu or a sudden sense of disorientation. Or, it can be a major disruption, a profound event that shatters our perception of reality. These glitches often occur when the matrix's programming, the intricate web of algorithms that sustains it, encounters a conflict or a paradox it cannot reconcile.

One example of a glitch in the matrix is the Mandela effect. This phenomenon occurs when a large group of people remembers a specific event or detail one way, while the documented evidence suggests otherwise. It's the eerie feeling of remembering Nelson Mandela's death in the 1980s when, in fact, he is said to have passed away in 2013. The one that really hit me hard is that the internet says that Ed McMann was never a spokesman for Publishers Clearing House (aging myself again).

I grew up watching endless hours of television and suffered

through all the countless commercials back before cable and live streaming, when network TV stations were our only option. The Publishers Clearing House Sweepstakes commercial filmed people who won and if you won, Ed McMahon came to your house with balloons and a big oversized check. To hear sources now-a-days say that he absolutely never did that is just crazy to me. I call bullshit. But google it yourself. There are numerous Mandela effect controversies that might resonate with you.

So, why do these glitches matter? Why should we pay attention to them? These glitches in the matrix serve as catalysts, nudging us to question the status quo. They provide a glimpse behind the curtain, a chance to grasp the reality that lies beyond the illusion. By recognizing that what we see and experience may not always be the complete picture, we can open our minds and begin to challenge the boundaries imposed upon us. We can expand our consciousness.

The Different Worlds of Our Reality

In order to follow along with the ideas presented in this book, you need to understand the different kinds of worlds that contribute to our understanding of the universe. The first world is the physical world, the material world, and can also be referred to as the "local" world. I often refer to it as *the matrix*. It is the realm we are most familiar with in our day-to-day lives. This world encompasses everything we can perceive through our senses, it is defined by matter and governed by the laws of physics, where atoms dance and molecules collide to create the intricate tapestry of reality.

This is the realm we are most accustomed to, the one we can touch, see, and feel. It is the world of tangible objects and observable phenomena. From the majestic mountains to the delicate petals of a flower, from the softness of a caress to the warmth of the sun's rays and further on to the vast galaxies stretching across the night sky. The physical world, or local realm, envelops us in its rich tapestry of sensory experiences. It is the stage upon which our human drama unfolds, providing us with the raw materials for our dreams and desires.

Beyond the physical realm, there is the second world, the subtle world or non local realm, you could also refer to it as the mental world. This is where our thoughts, emotions, and consciousness reside. This world is not bound by physicality; it transcends the limits of our senses. In this ethereal world, the laws of quantum physics govern the interplay of particles and waves, and everything is energy and all energy is interconnected in a dance of infinite possibility. The scientific community categorically recognizes the existence of the non local world but have yet to discover the best way to concretely study it based on the scientific method. It stands to be the next biggest challenge for the advancement of science and knowledge, and scientific theories have begun to emerge.

In this non local dimension of existence the mind plays a crucial role. Our thoughts and our intentions can become powerful forces that can shape our reality. In this world, our beliefs, perceptions, and desires deeply influence the experiences we encounter in our lives. This is where we go when we meditate and practice mindfulness. It is a realm where energy and consciousness intertwine. By delving into the depths of our consciousness and aligning ourselves with the energy of the universe, we can tap into this vast reservoir of creative power and profoundly transform our own lives and the world around us. The non local or subtle world holds the key to unlocking our potential and manifesting our wildest dreams.

But it doesn't end there! The third world can be referred to as the world of the infinite, or the spiritual world. In yogic philosophy it is named the causal world and is considered to be a blissful realm, transcending even thoughts of Heaven. Nothing physical or material can be found here. It is the ultimate source of all existence, the mysterious domain where consciousness finds its origin. In this world, beyond the constraints of time and space, if you can get there, you can tap into the boundless and eternal essence of who you truly are. Here, the interconnectedness of all beings and the universe becomes evident, and we realize that our individual existence is intimately linked with the unfolding of cosmic or divine intelligence.

The spiritual world or the world of the infinite correlates to the seat where God presides, the Eternal Essence, the field of Source Energy, and for Star Wars fans, the realm of the supreme Force, as in "May the Force Be With You". In quantum physics, theoretical scientists call it the quantum field, an invisible field of energy and information offering limitless possibilities to whomever can access it. It is where dreams are conceived and lived out, where inspiration fuels innovation, where imagination takes flight, from where the muses are summoned for artistic influence and the most pure love abides.

It is where we glimpse the extraordinary potential that lies dormant within us. In this mystical and infinite world, we can become co-creators with the universe, weaving together the fabric of our destinies. Our thoughts, beliefs, and intentions radiate outwards, and in this boundless expanse, anything is possible. Recognizing and aligning ourselves with this incomprehensible spiritual dimension grants us access to profound wisdom, unimaginable joy, and deep inner peace.

To review, the three worlds can be referred to as the local, the non local, and the infinite – the physical, the mental, and the spiritual -- or the material, the subtle, and the causal. As we explore and contemplate these three worlds we can broaden our perspectives and embrace the astounding reality that our journey in this universe encompasses more than meets the eye. Understanding these terms will aid you as you venture forth discovering the secrets to manifesting your wildest dreams and uncovering the science behind the art of manifestation.

A Few Words on Science

"The history of science is the narrative of individuals with new ideas that are proclaimed to be heresy." - Rupert Sheldrake

In reference to the above quote, Sheldrake has it spot on. Science seeks to explain our physical world, but science is skeptical. It wants to discover the truth, but doesn't want to get it wrong. When new discoveries emerge and seem outlandish, they are often met with doubt and resistance until the scientific community can verify them through empirical evidence.

As we explore the scientific theories presented in this book, keep in mind that scientific consensus on a proposed new finding doesn't come about until numerous and unbiased tests of the new finding can be replicated and confirmed. It can take even longer for a consensus when ideas or beliefs are not considered rational. And what was once accepted as a scientific fact can morph and change over time, from the gradual development of new discoveries and ideas. So, in truth, our understanding of our reality is always changing and evolving.

I hope to show you an immense accumulation of observable science and compelling phenomena that when considered together, will expand your knowledge of not only the physical realm but also the hidden realm of what is possible and how this all ties together when determining the validity of manifestation. And please remember, just because science hasn't found empirical evidence to prove something yet, doesn't mean it is not real.

The scientific community requires a significant amount of successful testing of a hypothesis to openly declare a new discovery as truth. They often drag their feet until they are sure, beyond a shadow of a doubt. There is a standard of scrutiny by the scientific community that guides their judgement of new theories.

The scientific method steers the process of objectively establishing facts through experimentation and testing. Scientific evidence relies on observable and impartial data and it is crucial for researchers to ensure that the data they collect clearly defends the hypothesis in question. But science is not 100 percent accurate. Theories are constantly tested and refined, and new discoveries can lead to changes in what was once universally accepted.

Truth sometimes emerges as a silly notion that is laughed at or brushed aside, and next it might progress to an argument that is scoffed at or hotly debated, and then it may move on to hysterical heights of opposition from society or religion, and sometimes to the extreme of imprisonment or death (think Galileo and Aristotle), but finally, somewhere along the way, that ridiculous new idea is accepted as obvious.

Historical Evolution of Science

Newtonian Science, pioneered by the iconic Sir Isaac Newton in the late 17th century, laid the foundation for our understanding of the physical world. Its majestic principles, grounded in classical mechanics, provided a blueprint for explaining the motion of objects and the forces that govern them. Newton's three laws of motion, the concepts of mass and gravity, and his revolutionary work on optics propelled mankind's understanding to heights previously unimaginable.

With immense precision and unwavering confidence, Newtonian Science, or often referred to as Traditional Science reigned supreme for centuries, as the unrivaled champion of knowledge. Yet, as the saying goes, "change is the only constant," and the dawn of the 20th century unveiled a world that defied the neat boundaries of Newton's universe.

Enter Quantum Mechanics, the dazzling star that shattered the scientific world, unmasking a reality far stranger and more enchanting than ever imagined. Quantum Mechanics, which came to be referred to now-a-days as Quantum Physics, emerged from the minds of brilliant thinkers like Niels Bohr, Max Planck, Albert Einstein, Erwin Schrödinger, Werner Heisenberg, and countless others who ventured into the mysterious realm of the infinitesimal.

In its most simple form, quantum physics is the study of tiny things. It is the branch of physics that deals with the behavior and interactions of matter and energy at the smallest scales. It is the study of the fundamental building blocks of the universe–the particles and forces we cannot see–that make up everything we do see around us in the physical world.

To truly grasp the concept behind quantum physics, imagine you are a detective investigating a crime scene. As you meticulously examine the evidence, you begin to realize that the traditional laws of physics, the ones that govern our everyday world, no longer hold true.

You discover that particles, such as electrons or photons, can exist in multiple states simultaneously. This means they are not confined to a single path, but can be in multiple places at once. To make matters even more confusing, particles can also instantaneously affect each other's states, regardless of the distance between them. Einstein called this phenomenon "spooky action at a distance."

This bizarre behavior of particles is governed by mathematical equations known as wavefunctions. Rather than dealing with absolute certainty, quantum physics operates in a realm of probabilities. Quantum physics revolutionizes our understanding of reality by introducing uncertainty at the very core of the universe. It challenges our intuitive notions of cause and effect, and opens the door to a world of endless possibilities.

One of the most iconic experiments in quantum physics is the double-slit experiment. Picture two parallel slits in one side of a wooden box, and light particles being fired at it. In classical physics, when we look inside the box, at the back wall of the box, on a screen, where we've captured the imprint of the light particles that entered through the slits, we would expect to see a simple pattern of two thin bands of light, exactly the same size and dimensions of the slits that they passed through.

However, in the quantum world, something extraordinary happens. It has been discovered that the light particles behave both as particles and waves. After light particles enter the box through the slits, they become waves, and thus the marks of light captured on the back of the box look more like intricate patterns of cylindrical waves. Instead of seeing two bands of light, the waves have created an interference pattern of multiple rounded bands displayed on the screen at the back of the box.

This experiment demonstrates the wave-particle duality of

quantum particles, where they can exhibit characteristics of both particles and waves simultaneously. It is understood that when these wave-particles are observed, the wave part of them collapses and they become just particles. Before the wave-particles were shot through the two slits in the box, they were observed, seen, by the physicists, and so they appeared as light particles. But when they entered the closed box through the tiny slits, no one was able to observe them because the lid of the box was closed. It was then that they shape-shifted, if you will, into waves.

The key difference between Newtonian Science and Quantum Mechanics lies in the very fabric of reality. Newton's laws treat nature as a predictable and utterly deterministic clockwork mechanism. Objects move with certainty in accordance with known forces, and their properties can be precisely measured. It's a world where a billiard ball striking another ball will follow an exact path, and the outcome can be calculated with precision.

On the other hand, Quantum Physics dances to a different tune. It reveals a universe where particles exist in a state of uncertainty, where it becomes impossible to simultaneously measure both the position and velocity of a particle with absolute certainty. Instead, we are confronted with a dazzling array of probabilities and strange behavior by these wave-particles. Quantum objects, such as electrons, can also act both as particles and waves. Electrons can also occupy multiple places at the same time, a concept known as superposition.

Moreover, Quantum Physics uncovers another enigma: the phenomenon of quantum entanglement. This peculiar cosmic connection suggests that particles once entwined remain forever linked, regardless of the distance separating them, be it a few feet away or across the world in another country. When one of the entangled particles is altered by some outside force, the exact change will simultaneously manifest in the partner particle, even though there was no observable cause for this change and even if the partner particle is on the other side of the universe. The implications of such a discovery challenge our very understanding of space, time, and causality, transcending the confines of Newtonian Science with profound implications for our perception of reality.

I don't know about you. But this shit blows my mind.

Objections to Quantum Mechanics

"The cure for a fallacious argument is a better argument, not the suppression of ideas." –Carl Sagan

The objection to the validity of Quantum Mechanics in its early days, ignited a spark of curiosity and controversy among the scientific minds of our time. Let me take you back to a time when this groundbreaking theory was just starting to illuminate the mysteries of the subatomic world.

One of the most eminent scientists who questioned the validity of Quantum Mechanics was none other than Albert Einstein himself. Yes, the brilliant mind behind the theory of relativity had his reservations about this budding field of physics. But why? Why would a man renowned for his revolutionary ideas show skepticism towards a new theory?

Einstein's primary qualm with Quantum Mechanics lay in its fundamental concept of randomness and probabilistic nature. He famously stated, "God does not play dice with the universe," implying his belief that the universe, at its core, was governed by fixed laws rather than unpredictable probabilities. Einstein's preference for determinism clashed with the uncertainties inherent in Quantum Mechanics.

To elucidate further, let me introduce another luminary of the scientific realm, Niels Bohr. Bohr, an advocate of Quantum Mechanics, engaged in debates with Einstein, defending the theory against his objections. Their famous discussions, known as the Bohr-Einstein debates, captured the attention of the scientific community and provided a platform for the clash of ideas.

The crux of Bohr's argument was that Quantum Mechanics offered a profound shift in our understanding of reality at the microscopic level. He argued that the very act of measurement or observation instantly determined the state of a particle, which seemed to challenge classical notions of causality and determinism.

As one might expect, the debate between Einstein and Bohr was far from conclusive. It continued for years, with each scientist presenting new arguments and counterarguments. However, the majority of the scientific community eventually aligned with Bohr's interpretation of Quantum Mechanics, recognizing its ability to explain phenomena that classical physics couldn't account for.

Interestingly, even though Einstein expressed skepticism about quantum mechanics, his work in the field of quantum physics laid the groundwork for future advancements. He received the Nobel Prize in Physics in 1921 for his explanation of the photoelectric effect, a phenomenon central to quantum mechanics.

The objections raised by famous scientists like Albert Einstein highlight the vibrant and dynamic nature of scientific progress. The clash of ideas, although initially causing controversy, fosters a deeper understanding and drives further exploration. Quantum mechanics, once scrutinized, now stands as one of the most successful and influential theories in the history of science, inspiring future generations to unravel the mysteries of our quantum world.

"If quantum mechanics hasn't profoundly shocked you, you haven't understood it yet." - Niels Bohr

EVOLVE

You and the Universe

In this section you will learn more of the basics needed to understand who you are and the universe you live in. This knowledge is a continuation from the ideas presented in the Preface, Introduction, and Prologue. So if you skipped those by chance, you must go back and read them first, otherwise you will be missing important elements needed to fully comprehend this section. It is imperative that you evolve in your understanding of yourself and how your unique powers interplay with the true realities of the physical world, the spiritual world, and the world of the infinite.

Chapter 1

The Untold Truth: Mastering Myself

"Knowing yourself is the beginning of all wisdom." - Aristotle

Understanding who you really are and delving into the concept of the soul is a profound undertaking that requires a careful analysis of both spiritual and philosophical principles. To comprehend the true nature of oneself, we must explore the depths of spirituality and the spiritual or non-local world, unravel the web of misunderstandings we encounter living by the standards of the physical world or the matrix, and examine how our consciousness has been conditioned and hinders our ability to recognize who we really are. Additionally, we must learn about living in utter freedom and how it pertains to our desires and the abundance that nature is willing to provide.

Who am I, really?

This existential question has plagued humanity for centuries. To answer this query, we must move beyond the physical aspects of our existence and explore the spiritual realm. As individuals, we are not simply our physical bodies, but rather multidimensional beings interconnected with the vastness of the universe.

It is in the non-local world that our true essence resides. Our authentic self exists beyond time, space, and the confines of the local or physical world. I've often heard people explain it like this: We are spiritual beings having a physical experience.

You should spend some time questioning your identity. We are not the sum total of our achievements, possessions, or roles in society. Rather, we are the witness or observer of these aspects of ourselves. Our true identity lies in the conscious awareness that underlies our thoughts, emotions, and actions. The true essence of who we are is unchanging and unaffected by the fluctuations of life.

One mistake that people make in understanding who they really are is relying solely on the physical and material world. Many individuals tend to define themselves based on their physical bodies and the circumstances of their environment, overlooking their true nature.

To avoid this mistake, it is important to understand and explore the spiritual world, even if you don't consider yourself spiritual or religious. By recognizing that our true essence resides beyond the physical, we can begin to understand ourselves on a deeper level.

Michael A. Singer, author of *The Untethered Soul,* provides profound insights into the nature of the *Self*. To support his perspectives, Singer draws upon both philosophical concepts and practical techniques. He highlights the importance of mindfulness and meditation practices to quiet the mind and cultivate an intimate relationship with our inner being. Singer's teachings align with various spiritual and philosophical traditions that emphasize self-realization and self-discovery.

He explains that your inner being, what you might call your mind, is not you. There are two distinct aspects of your inner being, but only one of these is you, the other is the voice of your mind. The real you is not your mind, but the real you can utilize the mind. The other aspect of your inner being is just your mind thinking. Since you hear it in your head, you believe it is you.

Who experiences the dreams at night? Who sees and hears and smells and tastes? This is the real you. You are at the center of your willful intentions. As you contemplate the nature of yourself, the only way to determine the real you, is to return to the root of your being.

If you can achieve the simple awareness of being aware, and become conscious of consciousness itself, you will soon become aware of who you are. This is the practice of awakening, becoming a conscious being, living in the center of the true nature of the self.

What is the soul?

The soul, an intangible yet essential aspect of our being, can be understood as the eternal divine spark within us that is intrinsically connected to the Source or the Unity Consciousness or God, the Universe, whatever name you give it. The soul is the seat of our consciousness, our true identity, and embodies our deepest desires, passions, and purpose. While our physical bodies may deteriorate, the soul is eternal and transcends the limitations of life and death.

The soul is often misunderstood and overlooked in our daily lives. The soul is not separate from the energy of the universe, it represents our eternal essence. The soul is not limited by our beliefs and identities, instead, it represents our deeper, eternal existence beyond the boundaries of time and space.

By exploring the depths of our souls, we can rise above the ego and access a higher level of consciousness. This process allows us to tap into our unique gifts and talents, leading us to live a life of purpose, authenticity, and joy.

Have you ever known people who believe that life is solely about surviving and acquiring wealth? Maybe you've had some of that in you. Having a beautiful home, a luxurious car, and a thriving career is not a bad thing to want. Yet, many people go through life focused only on material things or status as their only motivator. And many of these people do seem to live a life that is full and happy. Yet we don't know what goes on inside, in the inner world of other people.

It is a common narrative, a story played out and repeated all over the world, when someone, who despite material comforts, feels something is missing. Those who feel a deep yearning inside to understand the true purpose of their life are actually being called to this idea by their own soul.

Even if we are resistant to spiritual things, your soul may make you feel so uncomfortable that one day you find yourself recognizing the existence of a deeper essence within. What's going on here?

Understand, the self is connected to the soul. The nature of the soul comes from a powerful force of energy and this energy wants us, all of us, to find inner peace and fulfillment in the present moment, in this physical world, regardless of our circumstances.

This is why throughout history human kind has been on a quest to realize the purpose of existence and the true purpose of life. Through a gradual process of self-reflection, being open to new experiences, and connecting with and learning from others in meaningful ways, our soul wants to guide us toward true happiness and fulfillment in this life and the life to come.

Understanding who you really are and the nature of your soul is paramount if you want to learn to manifest abundance in your life. If you haven't put any work into this area of your life, I urge you to take the time to participate in the journal prompts at the end of this chapter.

By becoming conscious of our thoughts, emotions, and attachments, we can start to separate ourselves from them and recognize that we are not defined by them. We must reconnect with our inner selves, where peace, joy, and unconditional love reside. By doing so, we can tap into the limitless potential of our souls and experience a profound sense of freedom and fulfillment.

Understanding Desire

Like me, you may have grown up in a world that looked at desires or wants, as a negative. For me, this was a warped idea from Bible school lessons teaching about not being covetous. And I took it to heart. But *coveting* pertains to strongly desiring something that other people have. I now realize, that is not the same thing as desire.

Then there's also the *desire* of the original sin story from the Old Testament, and don't forget the Buddhist saying, "desire is the root of all evil". Desire has also been connected to the biblical "lust of the flesh" which is commonly connected to sexual desires and the desires of sin.

A close friend of mine grew up in a conservative religious family that heavily conditioned her beliefs and thoughts. She was taught that her desires were sinful and that she should conform to societal expectations. As a result, she constantly suppressed her true passions and dreams, feeling a sense of guilt whenever she pursued them.

It's not hard to uncover why the word *desire* sometimes gets a bad rap. However, desire is defined as merely a strong feeling of wanting to have something or wishing for something to happen. That does not sound bad or evil to me.

In fact all technology and innovation throughout history sprung forth from the desires of the earliest peoples to make the world a better place. This is technology defined, solving human problems to make life better and easier. So the idea of desire can and should be looked at as positive also.

Our desires are very connected to who we are. We all want to know how we can get what we want out of life. And we have all experienced that some of our desires come true while others don't. Why? What is the mystery of desire? How does it work?

Desire is self-fulfilling. If that is true then it's inevitable that you will get what you want. What you will learn from this book is that your consciousness, the *real you* we are talking about in this chapter, plays an important role in manifesting your desires.

Forming an intention of what you desire and taking action toward a conclusion is a mechanism of consciousness. You see, consciousness is always in play from the seed of desire to its fulfillment in this material world.

Elevating your awareness and discovering who you really are, the real you, is what enables you to live in pure consciousness. Your awareness is like a filter through which a desire must pass. Unfortunately, the inner path of desire is masked for most people who walk through life asleep and unaware of the power of their consciousness.

Look at it this way, the dream world is a non local world, a spiritual world, and we all have the ability to go there. In that world we are not physical beings, we transcend into a world where our real self gets to visit.

When you desire something in your dreams, it appears instantly. Consciousness as it operates in waking life, in the physical or local world, is meant to be exactly the same. The mechanics of desire takes place in consciousness. You desire something, you form an intention, and then you live in awareness by taking action, looking for signs and omens, paying attention to coincidences and unforeseen opportunities, until your heart's desire is made manifest.

Why do most people expect that their desires will not come true without hindrance or struggle? The simple answer is your desires can come true without unnecessary difficulties, if you let fulfillment unfold through consciousness. Yes, awareness is a maze of twisted turns that intentions must negotiate, but the advantage of knowing who you really are and what you really are, *pure consciousness*, is the secret to actualizing your desires with ease.

These ideas are impossible to accept for the majority of people who have been conditioned by the rational limits of a society that favors living in the dark. The information I am passing onto you can change your life. I hope you really spend some time contemplating the true reality of our reality. Alas, most people don't believe in the possibility that all desire is self-fulfilling, and thus desire and manifestation for most remain a mystery.

The Problem With Doubt

Another mistake people often make is doubting the abundance of nature, the universe, and the power of their desires. When we lack faith in the innate generosity of the universe, we create barriers that prevent us from receiving what we truly want. This mindset of scarcity and doubt limits our perception and hinders our ability to tap into our limitless potential. Instead, we must shed our conditioned consciousness and embrace a mindset of abundance and trust. By aligning ourselves with our deepest desires and having faith in the abundance of nature, we can manifest our dreams into reality.

Think about the strong feelings of desire that you are feeling in your life now. The question here is, where is that feeling coming from? Well, it is coming from you, the real you and your soul. You are uniquely you, no one is exactly like you and know one knows you better than yourself.

Once we have food, water and shelter, most of us still need safety, belonging and the knowledge that we matter. But beyond that, our desires are as unique as our souls are. I believe that when you truly understand who you are, your desires, those strong feelings, become a part of the flow of the Universe. Our desires are not whimsical or superficial; they are powerful forces that drive the creation of our lives.

But doubt is the enemy. Doubt will alter the course of your desires. Doubt will shut down your powers. Beware of doubt and push thoughts of doubt away if they creep in. The conditioned local world of limited and rational thinking will want to make you conform to its beliefs. You must fully realize who you really are, you must transform your destiny, by creating a new mindset, one where you are in control. This is the way to be reborn into the spiritual or non local realm. A world where miracles abide and become the norm.

"Do not be conformed to this world, but be transformed by the renewal of your mind." - Saint Paul

Conditioned Consciousness

When we doubt or lack faith in the innate generosity of nature, we create barriers that prevent us from receiving what we truly want. The cultural conditioning we experience from wherever in the world we grow up can color our perspectives and for many, as we enter adulthood, we have completely lost touch with our true self.

Living in the matrix, the cultural, social, political environments in which we develop, can confuse things and make us lose touch with our spiritual identity. These barriers often manifest as conditioned consciousness, shaped by societal norms, belief systems, and past experiences. Conditioned consciousness limits our perception and undermines our ability to tap into the limitless potential that lies within us.

Think of a person who has always struggled with limiting beliefs and self-doubt. They have a desire to pursue their passions and dreams, but their conditioned consciousness tells them that they are not capable or deserving of success.

Or consider a person who has always been driven by societal expectations and external validation. They have spent their life chasing success, wealth, and material possessions, yet they still feel empty and unfulfilled.

And imagine a person who has always felt a sense of emptiness and disconnection from the world around them. They yearn for a deeper connection to something greater than themselves.

Do you perhaps recognize yourself in one of these examples? You are in charge of your consciousness. It can be difficult, but we have it within us to break out of any kind of conditioned consciousness. Until you do this you will not be free and your power will diminish.

Healing from Trauma

Recent studies have emerged that indicate a good number of the population have experienced some kind of childhood trauma. Trauma is merely an unhealed wound. Whether the wound is extreme, physically violent, a long suffering hardship, a cruel form of mental abuse or abandonment, or simply the fact that you could never please your father, it doesn't matter. A wound is a wound. And wounds need to be healed. Don't reduce the impact of a childhood trauma that now, looking back on, as an adult, feels trivial.

I did this of course, wanting approval or praise from my father practically my whole life. Maybe you felt you were not seen or appreciated as a child. It doesn't have to be life debilitating, but the fact that you had to learn to cope with it, should tell you it was trauma. And you must do the work to heal your trauma at whatever level it affects you.

Experiencing any form of trauma or God forbid, an unfortunate experience of extreme trauma, and then not addressing it, but carrying the weight of it for years, hinders your ability to fully experience joy and bliss. It alters the potential of your consciousness and thus your power.

To heal yourself of trauma you must acknowledge the event, accept support, practice self care, focus on your physical health, practice mindfulness and meditation, journal your experience, and if needed find a therapist. Until you heal your trauma you won't be able to live in utter freedom.

Living in True Freedom

So what is our ultimate goal? What is it that we should ultimately create during our lifetime? What is it that our souls crave? The answer to that starts with Living in Utter Freedom.

If we live in utter freedom, it means we can easily make any kind of new choices in our lives at any given time without being constrained by anything or anyone in this material world.

Freedom means an independence from the operations of mass society and the pressures it instills. Freedom means embracing the realization that the essence of our being is intimately intertwined with the interconnectedness of the universe. It is about understanding that the universe is abundant and wants to provide us with everything we desire.

Freedom is about love, acceptance, forgiveness, positive life changes, perseverance in trials and challenges, vision for the future and faith. However, to fully access this abundance, we must recognize, acknowledge, and align ourselves with our authentic desires through pure consciousness.

Many people fail to recognize that living in utter freedom requires introspection and reprogramming our thought patterns. To confront these limitations and step into a state of utter freedom, we must shed the layers of conditioning and embrace a mindset of abundance, expansion, and trust. It is a journey of self-discovery and letting go of limiting beliefs. By doing so, we can align ourselves with our deepest desires and live in harmony with the divine flow of the universe.

I have always been a free spirit, but I didn't always flaunt it. I think that when I was younger, I was careful about who to share my true self with. As I embarked into adulthood, I really let my *freak flag fly* and I had no fear in being the rebel or the black sheep. Over time, I caved in to certain societal norms and pulled the reins in so to speak. This was mostly a result of being hurt by those who harshly judged me because I was different. I think they saw me as reckless and certainly as a non conformist, at any rate, I found I didn't enjoy being around people who were stiffly ingrained in conditioned consciousness.

Gradually, I learned when it was safe to share my true identity and with who. But if you were close to me and I trusted you, my free spirit would shine. I am now finally in a place where I just don't care what other people think of me. It's none of my business as they say. I embrace my free spirit! I can honestly say after all these years, I am allowing myself to live in utter freedom. And I am happier than I have ever been!

If you are just naturally a "free spirit" or know someone who is, then you can more easily picture what living in true freedom looks like. For some, this comes easily, but for many, it takes some work. If living in utter freedom sounds like a difficulty for you, maybe the universe will throw a wrench in the works to sort of wake you up. This might be in the form of the loss of a job, an illness or disease of a loved one or yourself, the loss of a relationship or being trapped in a toxic relationship, the death of a loved one or any number of unseen setbacks or hardships.

When life challenges us and we struggle, it can be an opportunity to examine our true self, our desires, our place in the world, and our future.

Understanding who we are at our core and exploring the concept of the soul, healing from past trauma, letting go of conditioned consciousness, and learning to live in utter freedom will make you powerful, happy, and hopeful.

We all must move beyond the physical realm of life and tap into our true essence. Only then can we recognize our desires as potent creative forces and harmonize with the abundant nature of the universe. Doing this will aid you in understanding how manifestation really works.

JOURNAL AND WORKBOOK ACTIVITIES

To help you on your journey of self-discovery and alignment with your authentic desires and the abundance of the universe, I have created journal prompts that will serve as a way for you to reflect and memorialize where you were at the start of this journey. I suggest using a new journal and commit to visiting it every day.

1. Reflect on your own spiritual beliefs and philosophies to gain a deeper understanding of who you truly are and the nature of the soul.

2. List any conditioned consciousness and the beliefs, norms, and past experiences that may be limiting your perception and obstructing you from experiencing bliss consciousness.

3. What truly brings you joy and fulfillment. What makes you happy? Can you list 20 things? How would you categorize them?

4. What are your strongest desires at this moment? Write down whatever comes to your mind. List as many as you want. Realize these desires may change as you continue through the book.

Chapter 2

Rewriting the Script: The Intricacies of Thoughts and Identity

"I think therefore I am." - René Descartes

Am I my thoughts?

No, you are not your thoughts. Thoughts are a natural function of the mind and serve as a tool for processing information, analyzing experiences, remembering the past, dreaming of the future and generating ideas. Like the lungs breathe the mind thinks. If you are not controlling your thoughts purposefully, the mind will produce thoughts on its own.

Sometimes the chatter in your head may seem incessant because the mind has a tendency to continuously produce thoughts. This endless stream of thoughts can sometimes be overwhelming and create a confusing array of mental noise that is disturbing.

Picture this, you are driving in heavy traffic, feeling frustrated and impatient. Thoughts start racing through your mind, such as "I hate traffic, I'm going to be late!" or "Why does this always happen to me?" These thoughts will only fuel your frustration, but it is common for many of us for these kinds of thoughts to come up.

Think about a time when you were feeling anxious or worried about something. Your mind was likely filled with repetitive thoughts, spiraling into worst-case scenarios and creating a sense of unease. Or have you ever heard your mind have a conversation with itself? Suggesting one idea and then arguing for another? The reason you hear conflicting opinions within your own mind is because thoughts can arise from various sources, not all of which originate from your conscious self.

Let's say you receive an email from a colleague criticizing your work performance. You feel a surge of anger and defensiveness, and your mind starts playing out different responses and arguments. Some of them even surprise you, (the real you) because you would never actually do what is being suggested. You might find yourself getting involved in a mental battle with the thoughts in your mind.

According to Michael Singer in his book "The Untethered Soul," thoughts can be influenced by past experiences, conditioning, cultural influences, and even random external stimuli. Hence, these conflicting opinions can come from different aspects of your subconscious mind or external sources that have left an imprint on your thought patterns.

However, the more you understand your own thoughts, the more power you have over them. So, don't believe everything you think, for thoughts are just whispers of the mind, not the essence of who you truly are.

So how do we separate who we are inside our heads with all these thoughts spinning around? The answer is simple. You are the observer of your thoughts. In order to understand the concept of "the observer" of your thoughts, it is important to recognize that your true self, or consciousness, exists beyond the realm of thoughts. The observer is the part of you that is aware of the thoughts arising in your mind. It is the silent witness that remains present even when the mind is active with thoughts.

Now this is not to say that the real you (the observer of your thoughts) does not think thoughts in your mind. Of course you do. The trick is learning to know the difference. As I am writing this sentence, the real me is creating and I am in control of my thoughts. If I stop to drink a glass of water and look outside my window, my mind may wander and thoughts may pop into my head that have nothing to do with writing this chapter. When you are writing, learning, creating something, concentrating, working on something, and you are very engaged, you are most likely in control of your thoughts. If this concept is new to you it may take some practice to learn how to tell the difference.

Once you cultivate the practice of differentiating between your thoughts and the observer, you gain the ability to detach from your thoughts and not identify with them. This detachment allows you to observe your thoughts objectively, without getting entangled in their content or getting carried away by their emotional impact. If you get carried away by thoughts and allow them to control your emotions and actions, your life becomes a series of knee jerk reactions and regretful outcomes.

"The primary cause of unhappiness is never the situation but your thoughts about it." - Eckhart Tolle

By developing a strong connection with the observer, you can create a sense of inner peace, clarity, and freedom. You are no longer at the mercy of the constant mental chatter as you realize that you are not the thoughts themselves, but rather the conscious awareness that perceives them. This recognition empowers you to choose which thoughts to engage with, and which to let go of, ultimately leading to a more balanced and harmonious state of mind.

In order to strengthen the connection with the observer, various mindfulness and meditation practices can be employed. These practices involve consciously directing attention to the present moment and maintaining an awareness of the thoughts arising in the mind. With consistent practice, you can develop the ability to observe thoughts without judgment or attachment, further enhancing your understanding of the distinction between the observer and the thoughts.

The chatter in your head never stops because the mind has a natural tendency to generate thoughts. The conflicting opinions you hear in your mind can be attributed to various influences and conditioning. Thoughts are not immutable truths. They are fluid and ever-changing, influenced by various internal and external factors.

What Was I Thinking?

"The moment you realize you are not your thoughts, you reclaim your power." - Eckhart Tolle

I remember when I first learned about this concept, that I was not my thoughts. It was a huge revelation for me. It was only about four years ago and I feel a little embarrassed that I discovered this so late in life. When I think back to before this awakening, what comes to mind is how much I truly believed in the power of my thoughts, but I really didn't understand how to master them.

One of my favorite quotes is "What you thought yesterday is who you are today, and what you think today is who you will become tomorrow". This quote is attributed to Buddha and it really inspired me. When I started teaching public school, I cut out large purple letters and spelled out this quote, stapling the sentence to one wall in my classroom. I wanted to teach my students the idea that they could become anything they wanted to be in this life.

I loved to find opportunities to share this quote with friends and colleagues. It was my creed and although my conviction to its truth was stalwart, I wandered around the chances and changes of my life for years, not really knowing how to control my thoughts. The quote was like a reminder to me that if I believed in myself, I could do anything, become anything. And I intrinsically knew that was true, but I never made any real progress toward my grand and illustrious inner desires.

So I stumbled around most of my life motivated to achieve but not really manifesting what I truly wanted. Don't get me wrong, I accomplished some wonderful things, things I am very proud of. Early in my teaching career I became a National Board Certified teacher, a difficult and daunting task. I was one of about five teachers to be the first to claim this status in a school district serving roughly 15,000 students. I was the recipient of several prestigious grants that educated me in the arenas of American History as well as GATE (Gifted and Talented Education) research and instructional strategies through the University of Southern California (USC).

From there I became a regular contributor of professional development, instructing teachers on numerous applicable pedagogy at the district level. I eventually ran the district's GATE certification program for teachers, and I was a mentor for new teachers through a program called BTSA (Beginning Teacher Support and Assessment Induction Program). I served as a Master Teacher mentoring student teachers for a variety of local universities, California State Universities, as well as USC. I was named "Teacher of the Year" by several different community associations and initiated cutting-edge programs and curriculum at my school site, including SEL (Social and Emotional Learning) and Trauma Informed Strategies, both of which have affected change in the classroom culture of public education. I was a lead teacher at my school site and was loved and supported by the parent community and the PTA (Parent Teacher Association).

Oh, and I also taught in the classroom the entire time, not always a walk in the park. Being a teacher is a very difficult and sometimes unappreciated job. Just ask any teacher you know. It can also be very rewarding and uniquely empowering, but there are days when you feel like all your energy has been sucked out of you.

I am just trying to paint a picture of how ambitious I was during my 26 years teaching 5th grade at a public school. The point is, I have always lived by the standard "Excellence in Everything", so I couldn't help myself. But teaching was never my desire. It started out as a way for me to survive in the matrix and during those years I was influenced greatly by the conditioning of societal norms that also prompted me to marry mostly because it was time. So I found a man that loved me, and we did the mortgage, the picket fence, the two kids, and the dog.

The joy and fulfillment of having a family was profound. But, being a mother was way more difficult than I had ever expected. I remember a period in my kids' early toddler years, where I almost felt resentful that nobody had warned me about how hard this job was, not even my mother. There were several other close friends and women acquaintances in my neighborhood who confided to me that they felt the same way.

Motherhood is a 24/7 job when your children live with you and even when they leave the nest, you are always on call. But despite this rant, I can't imagine my life without my two sons. It is such a precious gift to be able to create a life. And it is so rewarding to nurture and love them and try your damndest to shape their lives with good values and the kind of never ending support mothers are called upon to give.

I am so grateful that I was able to be a mother. However, motherhood for me was separated from my inner desires. Desires that lay dormant for a good twenty plus years of my life. So how does this all play in with this chapter, you may be wondering?

Well, I can not stress enough how important it is that you understand the concept that you are the observer of your thoughts. And I can not stress enough how important it is that you learn how to use this understanding in your life. Who knows what path my life would have taken had I been more aware of who I really am. I have done the work to let go of my resentments about the fact that I was living a good portion of my life on autopilot, like I was sleepwalking through life. I believe this is part of what makes teaching the ideas in this book such a passion for me.

You must put time into waking up and knowing your true self and being in control of your thoughts. It is the prerequisite for being able to manifest your wildest dreams. By developing a deeper connection with the observer, you can gain mastery over your thoughts and experience a greater sense of peace and clarity in your life. Practice and persistence are key to developing a strong connection with the observer.

Here are some benefits:

Reduced Mental Chatter: Your thoughts may be loud, but remember, you cannot control the thoughts that come into your mind, but you can control the thoughts you dwell upon. Sometimes you have to silence the mind to let the soul speak.

Increased Emotional Resilience: By detaching from your thoughts, you develop the ability to respond rather than react to challenging situations. You can remain calm and composed in the face of external stressors, making rational decisions and maintaining healthy relationships.

Enhanced Focus and Productivity: As you gain control over your thoughts, you'll find that your ability to concentrate improves. You become more focused, productive, and creative.

Eliminate Negative Thought Patterns: Addressing and transforming these patterns requires patience, self-compassion, and therapeutic support.

The key to living your best life is understanding that not all thoughts in your mind are derived from your conscious self. Recognize that the mind is designed to think but not all thoughts are valid or worth engaging with.

JOURNAL AND WORKBOOK ACTIVITIES

Practice noticing your thoughts. After each exercise, record your impressions in your journal.

1. Take ten minutes to sit alone and silently observe your surroundings, perhaps you are outside or at the mall, it can be anywhere that you predict no one will interact with you. Just sit and observe what's around you and notice all the different thoughts that come up. See if you can tell which ones you are controlling and which ones just pop into your mind.

2. Later, find a quiet place where you won't be disturbed for at least ten minutes. Sit or lay down and close your eyes. Take several deep breaths and focus on your breathing. Then try to focus your thoughts on being in the present moment. If your mind starts to wander producing random thoughts, bringing up memories or listing off your to-do list in your head, simply notice them instead of trying to forcefully push them away or suppress them. This practice will aid you in adopting the role of the observer. You watch the thoughts as they come and go, without judgment or attachment. Then simply redirect your attention to the present moment. By doing so, you can stay present and focused during the meditation, experiencing a sense of inner stillness and peace despite the ongoing stream of thoughts.

3. If you find it difficult to fall asleep because your mind is filled with worries and anxieties, instead of allowing these thoughts to consume you, practice observing them without getting caught up in their content. By acknowledging them without judgment, you can create a sense of distance between yourself and the thoughts. If this is difficult at first, try finding an app

on your phone for meditation. Choose a guided meditation for sleep, music for sleep, or even a bedtime story for sleep. Listening requires your mind to stop thinking, enabling you to let go of your troublesome thoughts and gradually drift into a peaceful sleep. Here are some apps for your smartphone that I have tried and like: Insight Timer, Breathe, Waking Up, Aura, Calm, Headspace, Unplug, Simple Habit, and Buddhify.

Chapter 3

The Untapped Power House: The Enigma of Your Brain

"The brain is wider than the sky." - Emily Dickinson

How powerful is my brain?

The human brain, undoubtedly, is a remarkable organ. It is a complex, intricate mass of matter responsible for numerous cognitive functions, including perception, memory, reasoning, and decision-making. The extraordinary capabilities of the brain can be attributed to its intricate structure, extensive connectivity, and dynamic adaptability.

To comprehend the exceptional nature of the brain, we must first acknowledge its structure. The brain consists of billions of neurons, specialized cells that transmit electrical and chemical signals throughout the nervous system. These neurons are organized into various interconnected networks, forming the foundation for information processing and communication within the brain. Remarkably, the average brain contains approximately

86 billion neurons, and each neuron can form connections with thousands of others, resulting in an estimated 100 trillion synaptic connections.

To gain a deeper understanding of the extraordinary functions of the brain, I have studied the work of neuroscientists such as Dr. Eric Kandel, Dr. Oliver Sacks, and Dr. V.S. Ramachandran, amongst others. These experts have conducted extensive research and provided valuable insights into various aspects of the brain, including cognition, perception, memory, and consciousness. Neuroscientists have explored the neural mechanisms behind these functions, using techniques such as imaging technologies, neurobiological experiments, and computational modeling.

Research and scientific studies have provided evidence of the brain's immense power and astonishing capabilities. For instance, advanced brain imaging techniques, such as functional magnetic resonance imaging (fMRI), have allowed researchers to map and observe brain activity in real-time. These studies have revealed the brain's intricate network of specialized regions, each responsible for specific functions. Additionally, studies on individuals with exceptional cognitive abilities, such as savants or individuals with eidetic, or photographic memory, have shed light on the brain's untapped potential.

The Brain-Body Connection

The brain plays a crucial role in communicating with every cell in our body. Through a complex network of neurons and signaling molecules, the brain has the remarkable ability to send instructions to cells, influencing their behavior and function. This intricate communication system, known as the brain-body connection, enables the brain to regulate and coordinate various physiological processes, including cell growth, metabolism, immune response, and hormonal balance.

At the core of this brain-body communication is the nervous system, which consists of the central nervous system (CNS) and the peripheral nervous system (PNS). The CNS comprises the brain and spinal cord, while the PNS includes the network of nerves spread throughout the body. Together, these systems facilitate the transmission of information between the brain and the cells in the body.

Neurons, the specialized cells of the nervous system, transmit electrochemical signals called action potentials. These signals travel along nerve fibers, also known as axons, and are released at junctions called synapses. At the synapse, the action potentials trigger the release of chemical messengers called neurotransmitters, which then bind to receptors on the target cells.

The remarkable interplay between neurotransmitters and receptors allows the brain to exert control over various cellular functions. For example, neurotransmitters like dopamine and serotonin play crucial roles in regulating mood, motivation, and emotion. They bind to receptors on target cells, triggering specific biochemical reactions that influence the cell's behavior and response.

Furthermore, the brain can also communicate with cells through the release of hormones. The hypothalamus, a region of the brain, plays a pivotal role in regulating the endocrine system, which is responsible for the production and release of hormones. Hormones are chemical messengers that travel through the bloodstream, allowing the brain to communicate with distant cells and organs.

The brain is a complex organ that allows us to perceive the

world, think, reason, learn, and adapt. It exerts control over our bodily functions, regulates emotions, and plays a crucial role in our overall well-being. Our brain can also adapt and compensate for various injuries or diseases, allowing us to regain lost functions through rehabilitation and therapy. The extraordinary functions of the brain also extend to its role in psychological processes, such as perception and consciousness.

The brain's ability to create and retrieve memories, process complex information, and perform intricate cognitive tasks like problem-solving and decision-making are awe-inspiring. Research has provided insights into the mechanisms behind these functions, including the involvement of different brain regions and the intricate network of neurons and neural connections.

Neuroplasticity, a game changer

Before the mid-1900's, it was believed a brain was a fixed and unchangeable organ, set in stone after a certain age. The idea that the brain was hardwired limited people. But in the mid-20th century, scientists started to challenge this idea. And what they found was that you can literally change your brain. You can actually strengthen its abilities. Scientists discovered you could change and adapt your brain even beyond the critical period of neurological development. In fact it can change and adapt throughout your entire life.

This incredible concept, known as neuroplasticity, has captured the attention of neuroscientists worldwide. Neuroplasticity, the ability of the brain to rewire and reorganize itself, is the key to unlocking our brain's superpowers and enhancing cognitive function. It is a remarkable phenomenon that allows us to adapt, learn, and grow throughout our lives. By understanding how neuroplasticity works, we can harness its power to improve our cognitive function and overall well-being.

At its core, neuroplasticity involves the creation, strengthening, and modification of neural connections, also known as synapses, within our brains. These connections facilitate communication between different regions of the brain, allowing us to process information, learn new skills, and form memories. Neuroplasticity occurs through a process called synaptic plasticity, which involves changes in the structure and function of these synapses.

Imagine your brain as a vast network of interconnected roads. Every time you learn something new or engage in a particular activity, it's like taking a new route or paving a new road in this network. Initially, these new pathways may be weak and inefficient, similar to a narrow dirt road. However, with repetition and practice, these pathways become stronger and more efficient, resembling a well-paved highway.

The process of neuroplasticity can be influenced by various factors, including our experiences, environment, and behaviors. When we consistently engage in activities that challenge our cognitive abilities, such as learning a new language or playing a musical instrument, we stimulate neuroplasticity. This stimulation prompts the brain to create new synapses or modify existing ones, strengthening the connections between neurons and enhancing our cognitive function.

Additionally, neuroplasticity can also be influenced by lifestyle choices and habits. Engaging in regular exercise, maintaining a healthy diet, and getting sufficient sleep are all essential for optimal brain functioning and neuroplasticity. These lifestyle factors support the production of growth factors and neurotrophic factors, which promote the survival, growth, and differentiation of neurons, facilitating neuroplastic changes.

It is important to note that neuroplasticity is not limited to cognitive function alone. It also plays a crucial role in our emotional well-being and mental health. By actively engaging in practices such as mindfulness meditation, deep breathing exercises, and positive visualization, we can influence the wiring of our brain, promoting emotional resilience, reducing stress, and improving overall well-being.

Moreover, advancements in neuroscience and cognitive science have unveiled the brain's role in manifesting desires or goals. The brain possesses an incredible ability to harness our thoughts, beliefs, and intentions to drive our actions and shape our reality. Neuroscientific research supports the notion that focused and positive thinking can impact the brain's neural circuitry, leading to changes in behavior and outcomes. By training our brains to reinforce constructive thought patterns and beliefs, we can conceivably optimize our potential for manifestation.

Neuroplasticity is a fundamental process that underlies our brain's ability to adapt, learn, and improve throughout our lives. By understanding and harnessing the power of neuroplasticity, we can unlock our brain's superpowers. By engaging in stimulating activities, adopting healthy lifestyle choices, and incorporating mindfulness practices, we can enhance our cognitive function, boost our emotional well-being, and live a more abundant life.

Is My Brain a Quantum Computer?

There is growing evidence suggesting that the human brain may utilize quantum mechanics in some way. According to Dr. Peter Kvan of the University of Florida, the field of physics can inspire the creation or use of new mathematical tools to describe phenomena.

In the case of the brain, quantum mechanics offers a way to describe how measurements affect the behavior of physical systems. For example, when we measure the location of an electron, the uncertainty of its position collapses, but introduces uncertainty about its momentum.

The mathematics of quantum probability allows us to predict how these tiny particles will behave as we interact with them. Quantum probability also has implications in behavioral phenomena in psychology and decision-making. As the brain is composed of subatomic particles, it raises the question of whether the brain itself can be considered a quantum system.

Ideas about Quantum Cognition

Have you ever wondered how our brains make decisions and form beliefs? Well, the concept of Quantum Cognition seeks to answer this question by using the language of quantum probability to describe the way people think and behave. Unlike traditional cognitive theories, Quantum Cognition focuses on how making a decision or answering a prompt can actually change our beliefs and preferences.

Imagine this scenario: You just had a meal at a new restaurant and someone asks you how the food was. Even though you have mixed feelings, you might simply say "it was good." This example shows how our uncertainty can be reduced when we have to commit to a stance. Interestingly, quantum cognition explains that making one choice or measurement can actually affect our later choices, judgments, or measurements.

This phenomenon, known as *order effects*, is well-established in psychology. For instance, if you ask someone how happy they are with their life and then ask them how much money they make or how many dates they've been on, the relationship between the two outcomes might not be very strong. However, if you ask these questions in the opposite order, you might see a significant difference in their responses.

One of the reasons why measuring attitudes and beliefs can be challenging is because it's difficult for us to understand multiple perspectives at the same time. This is because these perspectives may be incompatible with each other.

Quantum cognition suggests that people's behavior under uncertainty differs from their behavior under certainty. To illustrate this, let's look at the classic game called the Prisoner's Dilemma. When one player doesn't know what the other player plans to do, they are more likely to act in a cooperative way. However, if they are told about the other player's intentions, they tend to be less cooperative, even though the possibilities remain the same in both scenarios.

The study of quantum probability provides a fresh perspective on our understanding of decision-making processes. In classical probability, individuals are found to hold steadfast beliefs, unaffected by the questions or prompts they encounter.

However, quantum probability suggests that making choices can actually increase certainty. By allowing individuals to entertain multiple perspectives simultaneously, it offers a more comprehensive understanding of behavior and the brain. Classical probability theory does not account for the prediction of order effects, making it less suitable for determining how people behave when making decisions.

Dr. Kvan's research sheds light on the intriguing notion that the brain can exhibit behavior that aligns with quantum probability. He argues that the brain has the capability to represent phenomena such as superposition states, measurement collapses, interference, and order effects. Consequently, it is possible for the brain to function like a quantum system. This perspective opens up new possibilities in understanding the complexities of our brains and behavior in terms of decision-making science.

By incorporating principles of quantum probability, psychologists may find answers to puzzling phenomena in the field of psychology. The application of quantum mechanics can enhance our comprehension of the brain's behavior when making decisions, providing insight into the context in which these decisions unfold. Moreover, quantum probability offers a means to describe human behavior without constantly creating new rules to account for deviations from classical probability. Although it's not conclusive yet, that our brains function as quantum computers, the framework of quantum mechanics can effectively describe the brain's behavior.

The Quantum Brain

Another fascinating study in the realm of quantum computation focuses on the relationship between quantum processes and cognitive brain functions. Scientists from Trinity College in Dublin have proposed that our brains may utilize quantum computation to explore and understand the complexities of human cognition.

Through measuring brain functions and their correlation to short-term memory performance and conscious awareness, this study suggests that quantum processes play a crucial role in our cognitive and conscious brain functions. This groundbreaking research could provide us with a deeper understanding of how our brains work and potentially open doors to maintaining or healing the brain.

The lead physicist on this study, Dr. Christian Kerskens, from the Trinity College Institute of Neuroscience, explains that by observing known quantum systems interacting with unknown systems, they were able to determine if the unknown systems were also quantum in nature. This methodology eliminates the challenge of finding measuring devices for something that is still largely unknown.

The results of this study indicate that certain brain functions are indeed quantum in nature, providing further evidence that quantum processes are deeply intertwined with our cognitive and conscious abilities.

Understanding the role of quantum processes in the brain has profound implications. It may explain why our brains possess a unique advantage over even the most powerful supercomputers when it comes to dealing with unforeseen circumstances, making complex decisions, or acquiring new knowledge.

By unraveling the mysteries of quantum computation within the brain, we could potentially unlock new avenues for enhancing our cognitive abilities and revolutionizing the field of artificial intelligence. This groundbreaking research paves the way for a future where we can harness the power of quantum computation to further unravel the complexities of the human brain and potentially improve our mental capabilities.

How can I achieve Optimal Brain Functioning?

When different regions of the brain work harmoniously together, it can be said that your brain is in coherence. Coherence occurs when the brain's electrical and magnetic frequencies are synchronously aligned, allowing the various brain regions to communicate seamlessly. This signifies a state of optimal brain functioning. Moreover, coherence has a profound impact on your physiology and emotions.

Envision your brain as a complex orchestra, with each section, the prefrontal cortex, the limbic system, and the neocortex, representing different players. When these players are out of sync or playing different tunes, it leads to a chaotic orchestra producing dissonant sounds. Similarly, an incoherent brain generates scattered thoughts, limited focus, and conflicting emotions, hindering your abilities.

Now, you may be wondering, how does coherence aid in the process of manifestation? Well, coherence amplifies the power of your intentions and desires, acting as a crucial catalyst for their realization. By entering a coherent state, you tap into the quantum field of infinite possibilities, where thoughts and intentions have the potential to manifest into physical reality.

When your brain is in coherence, you unleash the full potential of your brain's electromagnetic field, allowing you to emit a strong, coherent frequency. This frequency is like a powerful signal that resonates with the desired outcomes you envision, drawing them towards you like a magnet. It is as if the coherent state creates a sacred space within you, where your intentions are transmitted with laser-like precision into the fabric of reality.

Dr. Joe Dispenza, expert in the fields of neuroscience, epigenetics and quantum physics, and author of numerous books including, "Evolve Your Brain" and "Becoming Supernatural", has conducted extensive research utilizing techniques such as meditation and mindfulness to induce coherence. Dr. Dispenza's practices center on cultivating elevated emotions like gratitude, compassion, and joy, which further enhance the manifestation process. When you radiate elevated emotions, you become a vibrational match for your desires, aligning yourself with their energetic frequency and attracting them effortlessly into your life.

So, how exactly does neuroplasticity help in attaining coherence? Consider these details:

1. **Reinforcement of positive connections**: Neuroplasticity allows us to strengthen the connections between neurons that contribute to coherence. By repeatedly engaging in activities that promote coherence, such as meditation, mindfulness, or cognitive training exercises, we can reinforce these positive connections and create a more coherent brain network.

2. **Pruning of unnecessary connections**: Neuroplasticity also plays a role in eliminating unnecessary connections within our brain. Just like decluttering a messy room, the brain engages in synaptic pruning to enhance efficiency and coherence. By focusing on relevant tasks and thoughts while neglecting the irrelevant ones (think "bad habits" or "unhealthy addictions"), we encourage the brain to prune away unnecessary connections and optimize its functioning.

3. **Building new pathways**: Neuroplasticity allows us to forge new neural pathways and connections, creating alternative routes for information processing. This capacity is particularly essential when we encounter setbacks or challenges that disrupt coherence. By engaging in novel and stimulating activities, such as learning a new language or playing an instrument, we can activate neuroplasticity to build alternative pathways and compensate for any imbalances.

4. **Emotional regulation and stress reduction**: Neuroplasticity is closely intertwined with our emotions and stress response. Chronic stress and trauma can negatively impact coherence

within the brain, leading to emotional dysregulation and cognitive impairments. However, by engaging in practices that promote emotional regulation and stress reduction, such as meditation or therapy, we can activate neuroplasticity to rewire the brain and restore coherence.

The attainment of coherence through neuroplasticity requires consistency and persistence. It is not a quick fix, but rather a gradual and ongoing process. However, with dedication and the right techniques, neuroplasticity can be harnessed to reshape our brain and enhance coherence, essential for manifestation because it allows you to tap into the immense power of your mind and unleash your full potential.

When your mind is in coherence, the universe becomes your loyal audience, eagerly waiting to witness the masterpiece of your desires.

JOURNAL AND WORKBOOK ACTIVITIES

Record the tips below in your journal. For the next few weeks, put a tally mark next to the actions you engage in, each time you do them. This will give you a concrete measurement of where you might need more engagement moving forward.

Tips for Harnessing Neuroplasticity

1. Learn new skills and information
2. Engage in creative activities
3. Exercise regularly
4. Practice mindfulness meditation
5. Seek out new experiences and challenges
6. Maintain social connections
7. Manage stress and anxiety
8. Take an alternate route to work and back
9. Find a new recipe and prepare the meal for dinner
10. Eat different fruits and vegetables that you usually don't
11. Find a challenging brain building game/app on your phone
12. Turn off the TV and put a puzzle together with family

Chapter 4

Energy is Everything: The Science of Vibrations and Frequencies

"If you want to find the secrets of the universe, think in terms of energy, frequency, and vibration." - Nikola Tesla.

Energy Exposed

All things in the universe are made up of energy. Everything around us, including objects, people, and even our thoughts and emotions, are essentially a form of energy vibrating at different frequencies. From the tiniest subatomic particles to gigantic galaxies millions of light-years away, vibrational frequencies are the unique patterns of energy that different objects or entities emit.

At the core of all matter, quantum physics affirms, you'll find energy in motion. Zooming in to the subatomic level, you can see that everything is composed of tiny particles called atoms. These atoms consist of even smaller particles called protons, neutrons, and electrons. They are not static entities but rather they vibrate at specific frequencies. Despite their size, these particles are always in motion, constantly vibrating and emitting energy.

Now, here's where it gets truly captivating. Each atom, each particle, has its own signature vibrational frequency. Think of it as a unique energetic fingerprint. These frequencies can range from low to high and they determine the characteristics and properties of the matter they constitute. When multiple atoms come together to form matter, such as a chair or a tree, their combined vibrational frequencies create the physical object we perceive.

But it doesn't stop there. Our thoughts, emotions, and intentions also emit energy and possess their own unique vibrational frequencies. This means that not only are we surrounded by energy, but we ourselves are energy beings, capable of influencing our reality through the vibrational frequencies we emit and attract.

By consciously aligning our thoughts and emotions with positive and high-frequency vibrations, we can attract similar energies or experiences into our lives. This idea was popularized years ago by the concept: The Law of Attraction. This idea was featured in the movie *The Secret* and the book of the same name. This universal law suggests that like attracts like, meaning similar frequencies are drawn to one another.

To paint a more vivid picture, imagine you are a radio station and your thoughts and emotions are the signals you are broadcasting. Each signal carries a particular frequency, and your experiences in life are like tuning your radio dial to a specific frequency to receive a corresponding station. If you resonate with positive, abundant, and joyful thoughts and emotions, you will attract circumstances and opportunities that match that vibrational frequency.

So, how can we use these vibrational frequencies to manifest our desires? It starts with taking responsibility for our thoughts and emotions. By consciously choosing empowering thoughts, cultivating positive emotions, and maintaining a high vibrational frequency, we become magnets for the experiences we desire.

Remarkably, you have the power to manifest anything by tapping into the energy that surrounds and flows within you.

One powerful technique to shift our energy and raise our vibrational frequencies is through the practice of visualization and affirmations. By mentally envisioning and emotionally aligning ourselves with our desired outcomes, we imprint our energy field with the vibrational frequency required to attract those experiences. This practice helps to reprogram your subconscious mind and tap into the creative power of the universe.

Incorporating meditation and gratitude into our daily routine is paramount to expanding our energetic vibration. When we quiet our minds through meditation, sit in pure consciousness, and express gratitude for all the blessings in our lives, we create an optimal environment for higher frequencies to flow through us.

Manifesting our desires through vibrational frequencies may not provide immediate results. Just as it takes time to build a muscle, it also takes consistent practice and dedication to align our vibrations with our desires. It requires patience, perseverance, and a deep belief in our own ability to create the reality we desire.

Show Me the Science

Truly, there are numerous scientists and physicists who have made incredible discoveries in this field, providing us with solid evidence of the profound impact of energy and frequencies in all things.

One prominent scientist who delved into the world of energy and frequencies is Nikola Tesla, often hailed as the father of modern electricity. Tesla's experiments with alternating current (AC) laid the foundation for today's understanding of power distribution. He recognized the fundamental importance of vibrations and frequencies, famously stating, *"If you want to find the secrets of the universe, think in terms of energy, frequency, and vibration."* Through his experiments, Tesla demonstrated the transfer of electrical energy wirelessly across space, showcasing the interconnectedness of energy and frequencies all around us.

Another renowned physicist who made significant contributions to this field is Max Planck. Planck's work in quantum physics revolutionized our understanding of energy and frequencies at the most fundamental level. He introduced the concept of quanta, tiny packets of energy that underpin all electromagnetic radiation. Planck's energy equation, $E = hf$, where E represents energy and f stands for frequency, unveiled the interplay between energy and frequency.

Enter Albert Einstein, the genius behind the theory of relativity. Einstein is widely celebrated for his remarkable contributions to physics, and his discoveries about the nature of energy and frequencies should be pointed out. Einstein's famous equation, $E = mc^2$, reveals the equivalence of energy (E) and mass (m), showing that energy can be transformed into matter and vice versa, matter can be transformed into energy. This profound understanding further emphasizes the inherent interconnectedness of energy and frequencies in the universe.

Furthermore, the Dutch physicist Hendrik Lorentz unveiled the concept of electromagnetic radiation, shedding light on the wave nature of energy and frequencies. By studying the behavior of electrons and their interaction with electromagnetic fields, Lorentz made significant strides in our understanding of energy transmission and frequency modulation.

Another key figure in this realm is James Clerk Maxwell, whose work on electromagnetic waves provided a solid foundation for the study of energy and frequencies. Maxwell's equations mathematically described the behavior of electromagnetic fields, laying the groundwork for technologies like radio and telecommunications. His pioneering work demonstrated that energy and frequencies are not only pervasive but also quantifiable and predictable.

Through their groundbreaking discoveries, combined efforts, unwavering dedication, and pioneering spirit, these scientific giants, Tesla, Planck, Einstein, Lorentz, and Maxwell have gifted us with substantial evidence supporting the science of energy and frequencies in all things. Did you read that correctly? All things. Energy can be transformed into matter and matter can be transformed into energy. You are made up of energy and matter. I am as well. There is an interplay between energy and frequency. Your energy emits frequencies. It can affect me and my energy can affect you. This is fact, backed by science. This knowledge offers us a glimpse into the infinite possibilities of utilizing vibrational frequencies to alter our own energy. The secret lies in embracing and harnessing the abundant energy that surrounds us.

The Science of Manifestation

When it comes to the scientific understanding of energy and its role in manifesting our desires, there have been several prominent scientists and physicists who have explored this fascinating field. One such scientist is Dr. Bruce Lipton, a renowned cell biologist and author. His groundbreaking research has demonstrated the profound influence of our thoughts and beliefs on our biology and overall well-being.

Dr. Lipton is known for his pioneering work in the science of epigenetics, namely the study of changes in organisms caused by modification of gene expression rather than alteration of the genetic code. His research reveals that our genes are not fixed and predetermined, but rather influenced by our environment and the signals we send them. This includes the energy we emit through our thoughts and emotions. In his book "The Biology of Belief," Dr. Lipton presents compelling evidence that our perceptions and beliefs directly impact our biology and can either enhance or hinder our ability to manifest our desires.

Another prominent figure in this field is Dr. Joe Dispenza, mentioned earlier, who has extensively studied the power of the mind in influencing our reality. Dr. Dispenza's research focuses on the concept of neuroplasticity, which refers to our brain's ability to reorganize itself and form new neural connections based on our thoughts and experiences.

Through his studies, Dr. Dispenza has observed how individuals who consistently align their thoughts and emotions with their desired outcomes can undergo remarkable physical and emotional transformations. He emphasizes the importance of cultivating focused intention, coupled with elevated emotions, to create a coherent energy field that magnetizes our desires towards us. For more than a decade, Dr. Dispenza has conducted thousands of hours of innovative research—observing common people doing the uncommon, measuring the results, and analyzing the data. The evidence demonstrates there is a clear formula for creating lasting changes in the body and mind.

Furthermore, the renowned physicist and author, Dr. Amit Goswami, has devoted his career to bridging the gap between science and spirituality. With a profound understanding of quantum physics, Dr. Goswami explains that at the most fundamental level of reality, everything is made up of energy and consciousness. He asserts that our thoughts and intentions can directly influence the quantum field, causing shifts in our external reality.

By examining these scientists' work, it becomes apparent that there is substantial evidence supporting the idea that we can align our energy to match the frequency of things we want to manifest. Their research underscores the power of our thoughts, beliefs, and emotions in shaping our lives and influencing the field of energy around us.

However, while scientific evidence exists, it is an ongoing field of research and exploration. The understanding of subtle energy and consciousness is still evolving, and further studies are needed to deepen our comprehension of these phenomena.

Nonetheless, the knowledge and insights provided by these scientists should serve as catalysts for personal growth and transformation. Manifesting through vibrational frequencies is not about wishful thinking or simply visualizing. It requires taking inspired actions that reflect your intentions and remaining in a state of alignment with your desired outcomes. It's a holistic approach that involves nurturing both your internal energy and the external actions you take.

By understanding the influence of our energy and aligning ourselves with the frequencies we seek to manifest, we can actively participate in co-creating our desired reality. Through focused intention, positive beliefs, and elevated emotions, we can harness the power of energy to attract and manifest the life we truly desire.

JOURNAL AND WORKBOOK ACTIVITIES

How to Align Your Energy to the Highest, Most Positive Frequencies

Pick one of these activities to do today. Map out in your journal when you can complete the other activities. These are just a few simple ways you can begin to increase your vibrational energy. Give each one a try and keep the ones that serve you best.

1. Go alone on a hike or a walk somewhere in Nature. Be mindful of the beauty you discover and how it makes you feel.

2. Create a playlist of your favorite inspirational songs. Listen to it while driving or doing chores around the house, or anytime you have a free moment. Notice your emotional state while listening or maybe even singing along.

3. Write several self-love affirmations on post-it notes and put them around your desk at work, on your bathroom mirror, or anywhere you regularly visit each day. Keep them there for a week. Make sure to acknowledge them and repeat these "power words" out loud if you can or just whisper them in your mind. But don't ignore them. Here are some ideas: *I am loved. I am enough. I am worthy. I am talented. I am intelligent. I am beautiful, inside and out. What I'm searching for is within me. I love the person I am becoming.*

4. Take inventory of your life. Get clear on what is working and what is not in your life. Do a brief meditation, just sitting with yourself, silently in the present moment. Take out your journal and write at the top "Please express to me what is in my highest good about (fill in the blank)". Make sure to keep it

general. Instead of asking about a specific job or relationship, make it more broad like, "Please express to me what is in my highest good about partnership, or purpose, or connections". Then spend 10 to 20 minutes writing down whatever comes to mind. This should be a flow of thoughts, without a plan, you don't need sentence structure, perhaps you'll draw or doodle, just trust the process and don't stop writing until the time limit is up.

Afterward, re-read what you wrote. Make a note of any significant revelations you glean from your flow of consciousness quick-write. Be honest with yourself and make a plan to eliminate or alter things not working in your life and to add attention to things missing from your life that you've discovered should be more prevalent.

Seeing is Believing: Why the Sky is Blue

"Color is the place where our brain and the universe meet." - Paul Klee

What is Color?

Imagine, if you will, a world devoid of any light sources, a pitch-black void where objects are undetectable and shadows reign supreme. Now, introduce a single light source, let's say the radiant sun illuminating the scene. Suddenly, objects emerge from the darkness, revealing their magnificent hues. But is it the objects themselves that possess color, or is it our powerful and imaginative minds that project color onto them?

Color exists, but only inside our heads. What you call blue is your own interpretation of waves of energy flying through the air at various frequencies. Color is only a perception. Color perception is not an inherent property of the external world, but rather a creation of our brains and the way we interpret the signals received from our eyes.

As has been explained, the universe is composed of energy at the most fundamental level. This energy is conscious and intelligent, constantly interacting with information. Color, as we perceive it, is a result of this interaction between energy and information.

Quantum physics's wave-particle duality may be what's going on here. When an observation is made, the particle collapses into a single state. Our act of observing photons as waves of light, determines the outcome and magically transforms them into the vivid and vibrant colors we perceive in our minds.

As we developed as a species, our eyes as a sensor detected different frequencies of light and our brains as a translator assigned colors so that it could help us find food and not be the food. In practical terms color evolved and our collective consciousness used color for survival at first. Over time our interpretations of color have transformed and elevated to give us the idea of beauty, perceiving a wide array of magnificent colors in almost every imaginable hue.

Light is composed of different wavelengths, ranging from the shortest, which for us humans appears violet, to the longest, what we perceive as red. When light encounters an object, such as a vibrant flower, certain wavelengths are absorbed while others are reflected. Our eyes capture this reflected light, and it is then transformed into electrical signals that journey through our optic nerves, ultimately arriving at the visual processing centers in our brains.

The brightest part of the sun's spectrum, what we can call the visible spectrum, is what we actually see. And you should know that there is a lot more spectrum out there that no living thing comes even close to seeing. It's safe to say that light comes in a lot of different wavelengths. Which wavelengths correspond to which color, or which can actually be seen, depends entirely upon the eyes of the creature doing the looking, and not really on any property of the light itself.

Here comes the mind-boggling twist: Within the visual processing centers, our brains decode these electrical signals and magically transform them into the vivid and vibrant colors we perceive in our minds. In essence, we don't actually see the object's true surface color but rather the specific wavelengths of light that were reflected back to our eyes.

Neuroscience can confirm that there is no such thing as color. There is such a thing as light. There is such a thing as energy. But there isn't any objective "real" color in the world. The coloring of the rainbow is nothing more than a shared, reliable, and consistent illusion that is a collective construct of the human race. Color is the computation that our brains make that enable us to extract meaning from the world.

In fact, all our other senses, such as hearing, smelling, tasting, and feeling roughly follow this same formula and are contingent upon our perception, so in effect there is no real sound, smell, taste, or texture to things we feel.

"Everything that is made beautiful and fair and lovely is made for the eye of one who sees." - Rumi

How do we see?

We have three types of photopigments, each of which has a different probability of detecting light at various wavelengths. One of the consequences of this is that we don't perceive a "true" spectrum. Instead, our brains have three values to work with, and they create what we think of as color from those.

There is certainly a set of wavelengths of light that most people in the world would agree is "red". However, that doesn't mean that the light itself is red, it just means that a human brain equipped with human eyes will label it as red. To get technical about it, there are receptors called cones in our eyes that act like little color channel sensors. One cone processes blue, another processes red, another green. An elaborate network of sophisticated cells in the brain compares the activity of these cones, and then signals from our brain produce the impression of colors.

We can say, without reservation, that a colorblind person sees colors differently than a colorseeing person. When a photon or light particle strikes the back of the eye, whether or not it's detected depends on what kind of cell it hits and on the wavelength of the light.

How we see an object has everything to do with how that object is illuminated. Our brains have adapted to see white as white whether it's under harsh fluorescent light or soft daylight. That's called color constancy. It's something that Monet played with all the time, painting the color of haystack shadows blue, for example, to compensate for the light that was illuminating them, but most people perceived his painted shadows as black.

Humans mostly see the world in the context of natural daylight, which is blue and orange, blue from the sky and orange from the sun. Those natural daylight colors are the context for everything else we perceive. They set the scene. They don't tell us the color of objects. They just illuminate those objects.

However, some animals have different kinds of cone cells that allow them to see colors differently, or see wavelengths of light that we don't see at all. Ultraviolet (UV) light has shorter wavelengths than visible light and thus us humans can not see it. However, many insects and birds can see into the near ultraviolet light. And many flowering plants use ultraviolet coloration to stand out and direct insects to their pollen.

Now that you know the fundamentals of how we see, it cleverly gives credence to the phrase: *I have seen the light!* Light, as it turns out, is all we see.

Optical Illusions

But what about the dress? Do you remember the photo of the dress, the challenge to name the color of the dress, that bombarded the internet and went viral? Different people saw the dress in different colors. If you never saw *the dress color challenge*, you must google it. The photo of this dress makes us question how we see, not just the dress, but everything.

As we look at an object, our brain automatically gets rid of the blue and orange to make room for the new color. Normally, our brains are adept at compensating for this changing light. But enter the dress. It's difficult to tell what level of light is illuminating the dress, which may be what's making our systems go haywire.

Our brain might tell us the dress is white even though it actually appears pink. But because we can see that the entire room is shaded by hues of pink light, our brains are adept at compensating for this changing light. If the room is under one light, say a yellow light, but the dress is in a shadow, then it is not being illuminated by that yellow light, and so it may appear blue-ish.

If you turn your computer monitor down, you might see it more as a dark gray and blue, if you turn your monitor up, it may look more gold or white. If you tilt your phone, you'll again see it differently, because you're changing the amount of contrast. Some brains compensate for the changes in light, other brains don't.

Color is perception, and the photos of this little dress, drives that home. It makes us consider something altogether non intuitive, that there's no such thing as white or gold or blue or black or pink or yellow. Optical Illusions like this illustrate the power of our perceptions. These captivating and often puzzling phenomena demonstrate the malleability of our visual experiences.

By manipulating the way light enters our eyes or how our brains process the information received, optical illusions deceive our minds and challenge the very boundaries of our color perception. They serve as tangible evidence that our understanding of the world is not fixed and absolute, but rather susceptible to the machinations of our own consciousness.

When we look at the dress, at that moment, the brain is entertaining two realities that are mutually exclusive. It's seeing one reality, but knowing there's another reality. So you're becoming an observer of yourself. You're having tremendous insight into what it is to be human. And that's the basis of imagination.

This little dress, it seems, is tapping into questions that extend far beyond the dress itself and have far greater implications. If two people see color so differently, what does that mean for how we perceive each other? What does that mean for how we perceive ourselves?

What this means for Manifesting

"Colors, like features, follow the changes of the emotions." - Pablo Picasso

We have learned that the wavelengths that are reflected determine the color we perceive. However, our perception of color is not simply a passive reception of light; it is an active interpretation by our consciousness.

Our brain, acting as an interpreter of information, processes the signals received from our eyes and constructs the colors we perceive. This interpretation is influenced by our past experiences, cultural upbringing, and even our emotional state. Hence, two individuals may perceive the same object as different colors based on their unique interpretations.

The insightful explanation of color perception unveils the fascinating truth that color is indeed a perception of the collective human race, a magical interplay between light, our senses, and the kaleidoscope of colors that we share in unity to enrich our lives. Our brains, in all their miraculous complexity, construct a vibrant, dynamic reality that reflects our unique interpretations of the world around us.

Our preconceptions about color perception, should urge us to reconsider the very essence of our reality. It implies that colors are part of our shared consciousness with everybody in this world today. So indeed, this is a mystery! Obviously, the energy emitted from our conscious being interacts with the energy of other conscious beings. Therefore, it stands to reason that within the laws of the universe, we are all interconnected and can communicate in a non-local way. This is huge!

We are also interconnected and intricately tied to the biology and workings of our extraordinary brains. It is our neural circuitry that imbues the world with color, transforming a colorless existence into a mesmerizing tapestry of hues.

However, studies have demonstrated how our beliefs and expectations shape not only our experience of color but also our overall well-being. For instance, research in the field of psychology has shown that exposure to specific colors can elicit emotional and physiological responses, influencing our mood, concentration, and even appetite.

Envision a serene and picturesque garden. The same vibrant blossoms may elicit different emotions and responses in different individuals based on their unique perception filters. Someone who harbors a deep sense of joy and appreciation may perceive the colors as more radiant and uplifting. Conversely, someone burdened by negativity might find the colors dim and lackluster in their perception.

Color is not just a physical phenomenon but also a reflection of our inner world. Our perception of color is intricately connected to our consciousness. As we cultivate a greater awareness of ourselves and our surroundings, our perception of color can potentially evolve and deepen.

Humans see color as a manifestation of energy and information and this provides us an extraordinary perspective on the interconnection between our perception, consciousness, and the vibrant world around us. By recognizing the power we hold in shaping our own perceptions, we can boldly paint our lives with the vibrant hues of our limitless potential.

Remember, the universe is composed of energy. This energy is not limited to tangible entities; rather, it encompasses intangible aspects such as thoughts, emotions, and consciousness itself. In this grand cosmic symphony, color emerges as a distinct expression of the vibrational patterns of energy and information. By embracing this knowledge, we can delve deeper into the mysteries of our perceptions and unlock the hidden power they possess.

In this light, the phenomenon of color perception becomes an invitation to explore our own consciousness and embrace the transformative power of our thoughts and emotions. By cultivating awareness and intentionally shaping our perception filters, we can transcend the limitations of our default interpretations and create a richer, more profound experience of the world.

And this, my friend, is exactly what one is doing when successfully manifesting. Manifestation of a desire is contingent upon aligning our consciousness with an acute awareness of the power of the vibrational energy in our thoughts, emotions and intentions, and this practice makes it possible for us to create and fulfill the desires in our physical reality. Just as we create the perceptions of colors.

Chapter 6

Connecting Us All: Resonance, Vibrations, Energy Fields

"The only source of knowledge is experience." - Albert Einstein

Our lives are built on our experiences and for scientists, observing nature and the experiences of all living creatures is how scientific knowledge is acquired.

Observing Experiences in Nature

Have you ever taken a moment to watch flocks of birds flying together in the sky? It can be mesmerizing to see the different patterns they make and how suddenly the group will seamlessly shift direction while keeping perfectly in step with each other. How do they know when to turn and how do they stay in such seamless unison? It's like watching a beautiful dance, yet how do they know the choreography?

As I write this book now, our dog, Boomer, seems content

lying on the rug near my desk. Yet, on countless occasions, I have observed him suddenly getting up and going to the front door to greet my husband. How did he know Bob was about to come home? But sure enough, in a matter of minutes, I hear the garage door opening and the car engine shut off.

One time this happened in the middle of the day. I followed him to the front door, expecting to see Bob, but I saw only the empty, quiet street. Returning inside, my husband arrived maybe five minutes later, greeted by Boomer who never left the entrance way, tail wagging happily, as if he sensed that his owner was on his way home. How did our dog know my husband came home to grab an item he forgot to bring to work that morning? He usually doesn't get home until the early evening.

A friend of ours tells a story about how he and his buddy were just walking along the street one day, when his buddy suddenly stopped and crouched over, clutching his chest in great pain. After the moment passed, and our friend had confirmed he was alright and no longer in distress, his buddy received a phone call from his father saying get to the hospital as soon as you can, your mother has had a heart attack! How can this be explained? Why did his buddy seem to suddenly feel what his mother was feeling at the same time and miles away?

Some of these observable experiences may have happened to you or someone you know. If so, I'm sure you've come up with your own explanation or you've accepted it as a curious phenomenon of life or settled on it just being a coincidence. Certainly, scientists are aware of the mysterious synchronization of flocks of birds flying. But guess what? Science does not yet know exactly why. There are theories of course, but no empirical evidence. Theories are what lead us to answers: Experience is the only source of knowledge.

The Resonance Of Sound Frequencies

The power that music holds to move us is undeniable. Whether it's a quickening of the heart during an exhilarating guitar solo or a swell of emotion evoked by a captivating melody, music has the ability to transport us to another realm. It can bring tears to our eyes, make our hearts race, or even give us chills. This profound effect can be seen across cultures and throughout history.

In many societies, sound waves and music have long been believed to possess the power to heal. From the Sanskrit chants of ancient India to the use of sound therapy in Chinese medical traditions, the idea that music can restore balance and promote well-being has been embraced by diverse civilizations. One notable example of music's healing properties can be found in the Gregorian chants of 16th century medieval Europe. These sacred melodies were believed to possess a transcendent quality that could alleviate physical and spiritual ailments.

Another fascinating aspect of sound therapy is the use of Solfeggio Frequencies. These frequencies have a long history but were forgotten for many years. However, in the 1970s, Dr. Joseph Puleo, a naturopathic physician and researcher, rediscovered them. He found them while studying the Book of Numbers in the Bible, where certain passages contained a series of six repeating codes. These codes corresponded to a set of ancient frequencies that were used for healing in biblical times. Dr. Puleo published a book in 1999 called "The Healing Codes of Biological Apocalypse" which detailed the power and healing properties of the Solfeggio Frequencies. Since then, they have gained popularity in New Age and alternative medicine communities and have become a part of the growing field of sound therapy.

Sound therapy works on the principle that everything in the

universe is energy, including the human body. By using sound vibrations, it aims to restore balance to the body's energy and promote healing. Sound waves have the ability to penetrate deep into the subconscious mind, activating cellular repair and treating issues such as chronic pain, anxiety, and depression. The human brain is an electrical device, and different tasks and emotional states generate different electromagnetic frequencies.

Sound therapy uses different frequencies to induce specific brain states and promote positive human brain activity. For example, the Solfeggio frequency at 528 Hz has been found to create resonance in DNA with healing effects, while the frequency at 639 Hz is said to stimulate communication and improve relationships. These frequencies can be played through various instruments, tuning forks, singing bowls, or sound recordings to facilitate healing and promote well-being.

The human body comprises various systems operating at different but unique frequencies, such as the heart, lungs, and brain. We are in a state of good health when we are in a state of balance. This state of balance is believed to resonate with different parts of the body and promote healing, relaxation, and spiritual well-being. Sound and vibration have been shown to significantly affect the human body, and this is the basis for using Solfeggio Frequencies.

There have been some studies exploring the validity of sound therapy, one such study examined the effectiveness of sound healing in treating physical, generational, and emotional trauma. Another studied the role of music in mind-body mechanisms, consciousness, communication, and emotion. It highlighted the significance of archetypal sounds and symbols in the subconscious. The study concluded that sound healing can be used successfully as therapy for PTSD (Post Traumatic Stress Disorder) and anxiety.

More research is needed to fully understand the potential

benefits of Solfeggio Frequencies and how they work on the human body. With new scientific discoveries emerging, we are beginning to understand the various brain states and the frequencies they generate and respond to.

Each Solfeggio tone corresponds to specific sound waves that have a unique effect on the human body, mind, and spirit. Here is a breakdown of the some of the corresponding frequencies:

396 Hz   Liberating Guilt and Fear
417 Hz   Undoing Situations and Facilitating Change
639 Hz   Connecting/Relationships
741 Hz   Expression/Solutions
852 Hz   Returning to Spiritual Order

The Solfeggio 528 Hz correlated to Transformation, Miracles, and DNA Repair has attracted attention by way of research studies that note its ability to provide tranquility and a source for relief of stress. Research has also shown that exposure to the 528 Hz frequency can promote physical healing on a cellular level. This is because the frequency is believed to stimulate the body's natural healing process, encouraging cell regeneration and repair.

Another interesting frequency, 432 Hz correlated to The Flow of the Universe is especially pleasing to the ear and said to reduce stress and promote emotional stability by putting you in sync with the heartbeat of the earth. Listening to music with a frequency of 432 Hz will allow you to connect with the universe feeling the power of the creative source. According to some music theorists, it's the frequency at which the universe vibrates and helps us to understand how we are creating our reality.

777 Hz is correlated to Calming the Nervous System and can be used to help people overcome fear and anxiety. This is because the 777 Hz frequency is believed to reduce feelings of

stress and tension. And then there is the 963 Hz correlated to the God Frequency. It is revered for its spiritual, emotional, and mental healing properties. It helps open the crown chakra, allowing us to access higher knowledge, deepen our spiritual connection, and invite divine wisdom into our lives.

The Frequencies of Bio Resonance

Humans are vibrational beings, and we share a magnetic resonance at a quantum level. The earth, in fact, emits a frequency known as the Schumann Resonance, which pulsates at a rate of 7.83 Hz. Our environment and lifestyle greatly affect the vibrational frequency we emit. When our cells and organs are healthy, they emit harmonious wavelength oscillations between 10 Hz and 150k Hz. However, when illness or disease is present, this normal function is obstructed, and disharmonious electromagnetic oscillations are emitted.

The communication between cells in our brain and other parts of our body largely relies on electrical impulses sent along neurons, which are electrically excitable cells. When these impulses are disrupted due to illness or disease, normal cell and organ function is obstructed, and disharmonious electromagnetic oscillations are emitted.

Stress-inducing and undesirable environmental factors like toxins, bacteria, diet, and external stimuli can disrupt the communication between cells, impeding cellular activity and leading to organic changes and physical symptoms. These changes have a direct impact on our bio resonance frequencies, causing them to alter. However, bio resonance therapy, pioneered by German physician Dr. Fanz Morell in the late 1970s, offered a safe and non-invasive technique to release harmful substances and inter-ference, restoring the body's natural bio resonance frequencies.

The early beginnings of this treatment holds its roots in acu-puncture. At the meridians determined by acupuncture points we find precise frequencies emitted by concentrated oscillations. Pioneering physicist Dr. Voll determined the individual frequencies of the nervous system are isolated at 100k Hz, the brain at 150k Hz, and the immune system at 67k Hz.

Bio Resonance testing has been used diagnostically to identify various allergies, asthma, and eczema. Certain spectrums of ra-diofrequency electromagnetic energy can have anti-tumor effects in certain forms of cancer as clinical trials have suggested. This method has also been used to successfully treat chronic insomnia using methods of biofeedback. Taken together these studies high-light the importance of electromagnetic energy fields and their impact on cellular functions.

There is little empirical data available due to the nature of double blind studies, for physicians delivering bio resonance treatment will always be aware of whether they are administering the active treatment of a placebo trial. However, other less rigor-ous evidence from studies examining the therapeutic impact of electromagnetic fields is promising.

Energy Fields of Emotional Vibrations

Emotions have a powerful effect on us and those around us. It's not just some abstract notion; it is backed by mainstream sci-ence. Emotions have a chemical, physical, and vibrational impact on our bodies and the world we live in. Just like a tuning fork, humans vibrate at a certain frequency, and this vibration is not confined within us. We emit vibrations that are received by others, and in turn, we receive vibrations from them. Our orchestrated interactions with others have a direct impact on all our organs and systems.

Neurotransmitters called peptides are responsible for carrying emotional messages throughout our bodies. These messages have the ability to alter the chemistry of our cells. While neurotransmitters are chemical in nature, they also carry an electrical charge. The electrical signals in our brains and bodies play a crucial role in how our cells interact and function. Receptors present on every cell in our bodies act as mini electrical pumps. When these receptors are activated by a matching molecule of emotion, they pass a charge into the cell, thereby modifying the cell's electrical frequency and chemistry. Similar to how cells carry an electrical charge, our bodies as a whole function like an electromagnet, generating a field that influences everything around us.

Our vibrations extend beyond the cellular level. When we communicate, whether through speech or other means, we send out vibrations through the air, which others perceive as sound. But there are other subtle vibrations that we emit, and these have an impact too. According to a groundbreaking study conducted by Dr. David R. Hawkins at the Institute of Noetic Sciences, emotions generate an energy field often described as a consciousness field. Using a technique called Applied Kinesiology, Dr. Hawkins assigned distinct frequency values to different emotions, ranging from shame at 20 to enlightenment at 700+. Fear and anger fall at the lower end of this frequency spectrum, while love and joy resonate at higher frequencies.

Understanding the energy field of emotions brings to light the profound connectedness we have with everyone else. Emotions are the key to this interconnectedness, as they shape our experiences and the experiences of those around us. Every interaction we have leaves a lasting impact, influencing change as we navigate through life. This realization brings about a whole new paradigm shift that suggests we are not alone in our journey, but rather intricately connected to the world and the people in it. Each emotion we emanate becomes a ripple effect that can change the world in ways we may not even fully comprehend.

The Resonance of Electromagnetic Fields

Every cell in the human body produces an electromagnetic charge. This means that we, as humans, are constantly generating electromagnetic fields (EMFs) that can be measured. Superconducting Quantum Interference Devices (SQUIDs) are the tools used to measure these EMFs. It is through these electromagnetic fields that information is transferred to our bodies, allowing all of our body systems to function coherently. Any changes to these EMFs can have an impact on every biological system within our bodies.

The heart, with its strong electromagnetic field, plays a guiding role in the function of all our biological systems. It is not just a pump, but the center of our being, physically, mentally, and emotionally. As bio-electric beings, we all produce electromagnetic fields, but the heart's field is the most powerful, followed by the brain. The voltage of these fields is difficult to quantify, but the electrical signals generated by the heart's electrical field can be detected using an electrocardiogram (ECG), with the average voltage up to 50 millivolts.

The heart's electrical field is stronger than the brain's because of its cardiac conduction system, which coordinates the contraction and relaxation of the heart muscle. Interestingly, strength and coherence of the heart is closely related to our emotional states.

When our heartbeat is influenced by negative emotions such as anger or sadness, it becomes disorderly and irregular. On the other hand, positive emotions such as love and happiness bring our heart beat back into order.

The heart also generates a strong magnetic field due to the movement of electrically charged ions within its cells. This magnetic field can be detected outside the body using sensitive magnetometers. The coherence in the heart's electromagnetic field signals harmony and organization to the cells and organs within our body.

The heart's electromagnetic field carries emotional information and communicates it through the surrounding electromagnetic fields of the people around us. Negative emotions weaken the field, while positive emotions strengthen it. Thus, our body's electromagnetic field is a complex interplay between electricity and magnetism, and it interacts with the environment.

Have you ever felt a sense of calm and ease when in the presence of a certain person? Perhaps their presence has a soothing effect on you, making you feel at peace and emotionally balanced. This feeling of wellbeing is not solely due to their personality or words, but rather it is a result of the interaction of their heart-generated electromagnetic fields with yours. Just like a radio antenna, our EMFs pick up signals from the fields of others, influencing the coherence of their electromagnetic field. This creates a whole new level of non-verbal communication, allowing us to transmit the benefits of our coherent heartbeats and EMFs to those around us.

One of the benefits of developing a coherent heartbeat and EMF is the increase in cognitive performance and emotional balance. When our heart and brain frequencies are in sync, we experience mental clarity, enhanced creativity, and better decision-making abilities. Additionally, a coherent heartbeat and EMF have a positive impact on our immune system, strengthening its functioning and improving overall health, causing a decrease in illness or disease and a reduction of stress and anxiety.

Our EMFs interact not only with the fields of other people, but also with the EMFs of animals, plants, and even inanimate objects. This has been explored in the scientific field of Plant Neurobiology, where research shows that the emotional state of plants can be influenced by the emotional coherence of humans.

Another powerful aspect of developing a coherent heart and EMF is the ability to enhance our intuition. By increasing our emotional coherence, we become more sensitive to the EMFs of others, allowing us to pick up on subtle emotional cues and information. This heightened sensitivity and increased intuition, enables us to understand situations on a deeper level, make better decisions, and helps us tap into the nuances in the art of manifestation.

As we develop a greater coherence in our emotional state, we naturally become capable of influencing the emotional states of those around us. Just like a person who lights up a room with their presence, the person with the most coherent emotional state has the power to tune the emotional states of people in their proximity. This occurs through the entrainment of hearts and brains, where the person emitting the EMF with the highest coherence automatically tunes nearby EMFs to the same frequency. This ability to positively influence others' emotional states is an incredible gift, allowing us to optimize our own emotional state in order to naturally assist and uplift the emotional states of those around us.

In recent years, more attention has been given to the research on emotions and their electromagnetic fields. Scientific studies are uncovering the fascinating connection between our emotions and the electromagnetic fields we emit. This field of research is gaining credibility and inviting further exploration into the far-reaching effects of our emotional coherence. By under-standing and harnessing the power of our emotions and their electromagnetic resonance, we can unlock our true potential for personal growth, manifesting, and the ability to positively impact the world around us.

The Resonance Of Morphic Fields

Let's get back to the questions about birds, dogs, and mothers that introduced this chapter. In 1981 Rupert Sheldrake proposed that there exists a collective memory inherent in all living systems, which he refers to as Morphic Fields. These fields shape and in-fluence the behavior and characteristics of organisms, allowing them to resonate with similar patterns and experiences across both space and time. This resonance is not bound by physical proximity, as it extends beyond physical limitations, explaining how synchronistic events can occur even when individuals are far apart.

When considering synchronicity in relation to manifestation, it becomes apparent that the phenomenon can be seen as a result of the resonance of morphic fields. Manifestation, in essence, involves consciously attracting and bringing desired experiences into one's reality. This process implies a connection between the individual's intention and the resonating morphic field, which allows the manifestation to occur.

In the case of flocks of birds flying in perfect synchronicity, this behavior can be explained by the collective morphic field that connects them. Flocks of birds flying together in perfect syn-chrony show a clear demonstration of non-local communication facilitated by morphic resonance. Each bird within the flock is attuned to the overall movement and trajectory of the group, made possible through the shared resonance of their morphic fields. This collective resonance enables them to fly in harmony, despite being physically separated. The birds' coordinated behavior showcases how morphic resonance can manifest a desired experience, in this case, collective movement.

Similarly, when a dog senses its owner's imminent return, it can be attributed to a morphic field connection established through time and familiarity. The dog's anticipation is not solely based on learned cues. The unexplained actions of the dog are enhanced through the resonating field that carries information beyond the immediate sensory realm, allowing them to sense their owner's imminent return. This connection beyond physical proximity demonstrates how morphic resonance enables dogs to manifest the experience of knowing when their owner is coming home.

Furthermore, the experiences of people feeling a connection with loved ones despite physical distance exemplify the reality of non-local communication facilitated by morphic resonance. The emotional bond and shared experiences between individuals create a strong morphic field connection that transcends spatial separation. Through these connections, individuals can manifest similar experiences or a sense of knowing when their loved one is going through a specific event or emotion. This phenomenon highlights how morphic resonance contributes to the manifestation of shared experiences and connections beyond physical boundaries.

All of Living Systems in Nature are Connected

According to Sheldrake's research, Morphic Resonance refers to a collective memory present in all living systems, represented by Morphic Fields. These fields shape behavior and characteristics through resonance, transcending traditional limitations of space and time. By exploring specific instances of synchronicity in various natural phenomena, we can understand how the resonance of morphic fields enables the manifestation of desired experiences. Let's look at a few more examples.

Plants have an innate ability to grow towards light sources, optimizing their energy absorption (tropism). This behavior can be attributed to the resonance of their morphic fields, allowing them to synchronize their growth patterns based on the availability and direction of light.

Ants, as well, exhibit complex collaborative behavior, with individual ants working in unison towards a common goal. This coordination can be attributed to the resonance of their morphic fields, allowing them to communicate and respond to stimuli in a synchronized manner.

Fireflies also synchronize their flashing patterns in a phenomenon known as bioluminescent synchrony. This behavior can be explained by the collective morphic field of the firefly population, allowing them to coordinate their flashing signals and potentially attract mates more effectively. There are numerous studies currently being conducted that are fascinated with fireflies trying to uncover the mystery of their behavior.

And even you and me as humans, creatures of nature, are susceptible to the collective morphic field, when we use our intuition or get a strong feeling in our gut. People often experience moments of intuition or gut feelings that help guide their decision-making. These intuitive impressions can be attributed to the resonating morphic field connecting individuals with their surrounding environment, providing them with a deeper understanding or insight beyond logical reasoning.

The measurable outcomes of these instances of synchronicity and manifestation increase our understanding of the underlying mechanisms and the validation of the power of consciousness in shaping reality. Being open to recognize meaningful coincidences in our lives allows us to validate synchronicity and confirms our position in the interconnectedness with nature. If birds, dogs, fireflies, and ants can get in tune with it, so can we. The collective memory within the morphic fields acts as a conduit for the realization of our desired experiences, bridging the gap between intention and manifestation.

Science is as Scientist Make It

Initially Sheldrake's theories experienced acclaim but shortly after the scientific community largely dismissed and met Rupert Sheldrake's theory with dogmatic skepticism. His ideas were viewed as scientific heresy and were simply ignored by mainstream science. This reaction highlights some fundamental problems with the scientific community, where powerful taboos dictate what scientists can legitimately investigate.

However, Sheldrake found a different reception in India, where his Indian colleagues affirmed that there was nothing new in his theories. They claimed that this knowledge was known to the ancient rishis, millennia ago. Sheldrake's work has also been connected to similarities with Carl Jung's collective unconscious theory, suggesting that collective memories can be shared non-locally among individuals.

It is unfortunate that Sheldrake's ideas were heavily criticized instead of being open to exploration and further investigation forty years ago. Certainly there is no shortage of unsolved phenomena in science, and Sheldrake's theories offer alternative perspectives that could potentially shed light on these mysteries. If you search the internet, you will find a substantial amount of arguments on both sides regarding Sheldrake's theories.

Despite the criticism and ostracization Sheldrake faced from the scientific community, there has been a renewed interest in his theories in recent years. This testament to the ongoing debate and interest surrounding his work acknowledges that his theory has gained traction and is being revisited by a wider audience.

As you will see in the next two chapters, current research is actively exploring the idea that our cells exhibit consciousness, memory, and non local communication. These new theories resemble the properties of morphic fields, just saying.

On an individual level, the understanding of morphic resonance and synchronicity gives us insights into the mechanisms through which manifestation can occur and should empower us to manifest our desires and make conscious choices. On a broader scale, the acceptance and integration of these concepts within mainstream science could lead to a paradigm shift in the way we perceive reality and our interconnectedness with the world.

My biggest piece of advice for you, is to pay attention to coincidences and synchronicities and trust your intuition, as they can guide you towards opportunities and connections that align with your desires. By harnessing the energy of your desires you can align yourself with the synchronicities of the universe. Above all learn to trust the connectedness of all living beings and embrace the possibility that our thoughts can shape reality.

JOURNAL AND WORKBOOK ACTIVITIES

1. Label a page in your journal as SYNCHRONICITIES AND COINCIDENCES.

2. Reflect and jot down any moments in your life where you felt the power of synchronicity through coincidences, intuition, gut feelings, or unexplainable connections or experiences with a friend or loved one across some distance.

3. Journal Prompts to frame your thinking: If you can answer yes to any of the following questions, revisit that memory and record what you remember from the experience.

   • Have you ever thought about someone and in that moment they called you or you ran into them, etc.?

   • Have you ever experienced a coincidence that you immediately recognized as a rare and telling message or opportunity specific to your life?

   • Have you ever had a gut feeling that turned out to be true?

   • Have you ever felt a strong connection to someone who was far from you and did you come to find a reason for it that can't be explained rationally?

   • Have you ever just intuitively known the outcome of something before it happened?

Chapter 7

Spooky Action in my Cells: Can You Believe It?

"What lies behind us and what lies before us are tiny matters compared to what lies within us." - Ralph Waldo Emerson

A Single Cell is a Tiny Human Body

Cell communication is a fascinating aspect of cellular biology, as it plays a crucial role in the functioning of the cell. The cell is the simplest form of life, yet it is capable of performing a vast range of functions. Within the cell, there are subcellular structures called organelles, which are similar to organs in the human body. These organelles interact with each other, just like organs interact within the human body.

This communication between organelles helps the cell carry out its various functions with purpose. The communication process in cells needs to be highly effective for the human body to function properly. When noise, interference, or misinformation enter the cellular communication process, the human body suffers.

The complexity of the human body can be compared to the complexity of a single cell. A human body consists of approximately 100 trillion cells, each containing around 100 trillion atoms. The physiological systems in both the human body and the cell are remarkably similar. In fact, the cell has its own boundary layer akin to our skin, a nervous system, a digestive system, an excretory system, a respiratory system, and even a reproductive system.

Cells Have Memories?

Recent research focuses on the memory content and non-local interconnectedness of cells. Physics experiments have shown that nature exhibits "implausible" non-locality, and this phenomenon is now considered a part of physical reality. In fact, a recent experiment demonstrated non-local quantum correlations over a distance of almost seven miles, suggesting that there is no limit to the distance over which non-local effects can occur in theory.

As such, the medical profession is increasingly aware that the cellular structure of transplanted organs carries a memory content to a degree never before considered possible. This research has been extensively covered in a number of books and articles.

An intriguing example of cellular memory is seen in heart transplant recipients. After surgery, recipients sometimes experience dramatic changes in their food preferences and musical tastes, even using words they never spoke before.

In one notable case, a heart recipient received a donor heart from a man who used the word "copacetic" as a code word with his wife. The heart recipient suddenly and mysteriously started using this unfamiliar word in a similar manner, although it was never part of his normal diction.

There was also a case involving a 35-year-old female heart transplant recipient who suddenly developed a greatly expanded interest in sex, with her sexual activities changing. It was later discovered that she had received the heart of a 24-year-old prostitute, shedding light on the intimate experiences and memories that can be carried within cellular structures.

Another heart transplant study brought attention to the fascinating concept of cellular memory. In this case, an 8-year-old girl received the heart of a murdered ten-year-old. After the transplant, the girl started screaming at night, plagued by dreams of the man who had murdered her donor. Fortunately, the police were able to use the descriptions provided by the little girl to track down the murderer and bring him to justice. This incident highlights the possibility that organs in our body have a cellular memory, allowing them to retain information and react to external stimuli.

The Cells of Twins

The communication of cells is a fascinating field of study that continues to reveal intriguing mysteries. One such mystery revolves around identical twins who have been raised apart. Despite their different environments, there are often strong clues that suggest a deeper connection between these separated twins. Personal characteristics, religious attitudes, job satisfaction, and even antisocial behavior show remarkable similarities that cannot be solely attributed to the environment they were raised in.

Personality studies conducted on identical twins reared apart have provided valuable evidence that suggests powerful convergent factors are at play throughout their entire lives. These factors go beyond genetic influences and environmental upbringing. While the technical literature primarily attributes these correlations to a genetic contribution, there is another intriguing element at play. Close coupling at birth, where identical twins share the same DNA patterns, leads to strong non-local influences between their brain and body systems. This additional factor adds complexity to the genetic and environmental factors customarily considered.

One basis for unexplained phenomena observed in reunited twins is the interconnected use of symbols and patterns. For instance, it is quite astonishing how often these twins have similar names. Take the example of two adopted infants both named Jim by their adoptive parents. When they were reunited at the age of 39, they discovered a trail of uncanny similarities in their lives. Both had dogs named Toy, married and divorced women named Linda, and entered second marriages with women named Betty. Even their sons had remarkably similar names, James Allan and James Alan, respectively. Similar coincidences were found in other pairs of twins, such as Bridget and Dorothy, who named their sons Richard Andrew and Andrew Richard, respectively, and their daughters Catherine Louise and Karen Louise. The likelihood of such coincidences is lessened by the fact that names are often joint decisions between husbands and wives.

Perhaps the most bewitching aspect of these findings is that they go beyond mere coincidences in names. Even in cases where twins have had no contact since a very young age, they have shared nicknames. In the case of Berta and Herta, both twins had the same nickname of "Pussy," despite living on different continents and not having met since the age of four. These parallels between reunited twins are a bit eerie, but remarkable nonetheless, and leave us captivated by the hidden connections between them.

Cells and Non Local Communication

To truly understand the communication of cells, we must recognize that the shape and spectrum of frequencies of molecules are far more complex than modern science once suspected. Subtleties exist at the cellular level, and these intricacies play a crucial role in non-local interactions. The communication between cells surpasses simple genetic and environmental factors, revealing a deeper web of connections that science is only beginning to unravel.

In the vast realm of cellular communication, mental thoughts hold a significant function in what could be deemed as a pre-space. Beyond the confinements of our three-dimensional space and linear time, thoughts serve as a representation of non-local inputs. However, in order for these non-local inputs to be effectively transmitted and understood within the physical realm, they must undergo a conversion process into symbols. This conversion allows for the translation of abstract thoughts into tangible forms that can be comprehended and shared with others.

It is worth noting that there are individuals who devote their lives to obtaining and harnessing such non-local input. These individuals often emerge as artists, musicians, poets, and even prophets like Moses, Jesus, Mohammed, and Buddha. They possess an inherent ability to tap into the deeper realms of thought and connect with a higher consciousness. Just as the cells of a person strive to function in harmony with the whole, these remarkable individuals serve as conduits for translating and expressing the essence of non-local thoughts to promote understanding, inspiration, and unity.

To truly comprehend the intricate communication processes within cells, it becomes evident that unconditional love at the cellular level is paramount for achieving harmony. Cells function optimally when they operate in a state of unconditional love, where there is a profound sense of interconnectedness and mutual support. In this state, cells work harmoniously together, supporting and nurturing one another. By embracing this concept, we unlock the potential for improved cellular communication and overall biological functioning, leading to enhanced physical and emotional well-being.

Given the profound implications of this cellular communication and the importance of unconditional love, it becomes evident that an expanded scientific paradigm is needed. Traditional scientific frameworks often neglect the spiritual and metaphysical aspects of our existence, limiting our understanding of the intricate interplay between thoughts, emotions, and our physical being. Embracing a more holistic approach that takes into account both the physical and non-physical realms could unlock groundbreaking insights into the communication processes of our cells and ultimately shape a more comprehensive understanding of human existence.

Bio-Communication of Cells

Cleve Backster, a former interrogation specialist turned polygraph expert, conducted groundbreaking experiments in the 1960s that provided intriguing insights into the potential communication abilities of cells and their potential consciousness. His primary methodology involved measuring the electrical responses of plants and other living organisms, and his findings sparked both interest and skepticism within the scientific community.

Backster's most famous experiment, which he conducted in 1966, involved attaching polygraph electrodes to a Dracaena fragrans plant, commonly known as a *corn plant*. His intent was to measure its response to various stimuli. Initially, Backster simply watered the plant and observed the expected electrical response corresponding to the introduction of moisture. However, what followed next was unexpected and extraordinary.

As Backster prepared to measure the plant's response to water, he found himself contemplating harming it out of curiosity. In that very moment, the polygraph recordings indicated a surge in electrical activity similar to what would be observed in a human experiencing a distressing situation. Intriguingly, it seemed as if the plant had somehow sensed Backster's intentions and responded accordingly, suggesting some form of perception or consciousness.

Further experiments by Backster revealed additional intriguing findings. He discovered that plants could exhibit responses to the thoughts and intentions of not only human beings but also other living organisms in their vicinity. For example, when he threatened to burn one of the plant's leaves, the polygraph recordings showcased a significant electrical reaction. It is interesting to note that his findings are similar to the beliefs of Hindus and Buddhists, who are known to revere elements of nature. It is believed that the Supreme Divinity is present in each and every element of nature.

While Backster's findings are fascinating, they have been met with considerable skepticism in the scientific community. Mainstream science at the time, argued that the electrical responses observed by Backster could be attributed to various factors unrelated to conscious cellular communication, such as changes in temperature or humidity. They also raise concerns about the lack of proper controls in his experiments and the potential for biased interpretation of results.

Despite the skepticism, Backster's work has sparked a renewed interest in exploring the potential interconnectedness between living organisms and the environment in which they reside. The field of plant neurobiology, for instance, has emerged as a discipline that investigates the complex signaling and communication systems within plants.

We know plants don't have nervous systems, but they do have little electrical currents flowing through them and are subject to outside manipulation. Furthermore plants can show altered electrical responses to light, chemical agents and disease. This growing body of research suggests that plants may possess sophisticated mechanisms for sensing and responding to their surroundings.

Cells Demand Sincere Intention?

This research underscores the importance of spontaneity and sincere intention in cell communication. Backster observed that both plants and human cells possess the ability to discriminate between genuine thoughts and those that lack sincerity. This highlights the paramount role of intention in cellular interactions, which poses a challenge for scientific protocols that rely on pre-determined instructions. If cells are informed of what will happen beforehand, the element of spontaneity is lost, potentially impacting the authenticity of the observed responses. Consequently, the exploration of thought discrimination in cellular communication necessitates support from the field of physics research.

The experiments conducted by Dr. L. Mandel at the University of Rochester challenge the prevalent view of physics by suggesting that mental acts can influence future events. The data from these experiments indicate that the possibility of an experimentalist taking certain actions, even if they do not actually take them, can still influence the results. This challenges the notion that events are solely based on what is, instead suggesting that they can also be influenced by what could be. Additionally, recent research on quantum mechanical complementarity reveals that the existence of information about an entity's path can cause its wave nature to disappear, further supporting the idea that mental acts can affect the outcome of experiments.

Dr. Glen Rein's experiments on the effects of focused love provide further evidence that intention and focused energy can influence the shape of DNA molecules. By holding a beaker with a test tube containing DNA samples, individuals in a state of deeply focused love were able to produce coherent ECG spectra, resulting in changes in the conformation of DNA. These changes were observed to be beyond what would be expected from maximum thermal and mechanical perturbation, suggesting a non-electromagnetic information carrier is at play. Furthermore, long-distance studies conducted at 0.5 miles away from the test area also demonstrated that intention coupled with coherent heart energy can cause DNA shape changes. These findings provide support for the possibility of non-local input at the molecular level, indicating that there are interconnected patterns and symbols in the world that science has yet to fully understand.

In an exploratory experiment, three DNA samples were simultaneously exposed to a focused intention of causing different effects in two of the samples while leaving the third sample unchanged. The results of this experiment showed increased absorption peaks in the two samples that were intended to change, while the absorption peaks of the third sample remained unaffected. This suggests that focused intention can act as a non-electromagnetic information carrier, capable of producing specific effects in DNA molecules.

Isolating Human Cells

One of Backster's notable experiments in 1972 involved isolating human cells from the individual they belonged to and measuring their electromagnetic activity. His pioneering work demonstrated the bio-communication ability of cells and revealed the existence of cellular consciousness.

Backster conducted experiments involving human cells. He isolated cells, particularly sperm and white blood cells, from human subjects and placed them in separate containers while still being electrically connected to the subjects. Backster then subjected the subjects to various emotional stimuli and monitored the electrical activity of the isolated cells.

Surprisingly, through the use of sensitive recording equipment Backster observed that the cells exhibited detectable electromagnetic responses that correlated with the emotional states of the subjects, even though there was physical separation between the cells and the subjects' bodies. This experiment suggested that there may be a low-level electromagnetic communication between cells and the larger biological system of an individual and implies that cells possess a consciousness that is interconnected and influenced by the emotional and psychological states of the organism to which they belong.

Cells Have a 6th Sense?

Cleve Backster also proposed that not only single cell organisms but also the cells of complete organisms possess a form of knowledge or perception. Backster's research focused on white cells from the mouth's roof, as well as human spermatozoa and other cell clusters. His findings indicated that cells have a "primary perception" that is more fundamental than our five basic senses. This primary perception allows cells to react to thoughts, particularly those that carry high emotions or thoughts related to life or death. It suggests that our liver cells, artery cells, heart cells, kidney cells, and so on can potentially know and respond to our thoughts and emotions.

Backster's extensive research on cell communication has led to groundbreaking experiments conducted over long distances. One notable example is the collaboration with Dr. Brian O'Leary, a NASA scientist-astronaut, who conducted experiments both in the laboratory and over a distance of 350 miles using his own donated white blood cells. Surprisingly, these experiments showed no reduction in signal strength, suggesting that cellular communication can occur without limitations imposed by distance.

Further research conducted at the California Institute for Human Research in Encinitas in March 1998 yielded similar results. Backster utilized a sophisticated magnetically and electrically shielded room to record the reactions of a philodendron plant and bacterial culture. Intriguingly, neither distance nor shielding appeared to inhibit the communication between these cells. Backster hypothesized that non-local input to cells was responsible for this phenomenon. He proposed a non-local input model, which suggests a continuum of intelligence that fills all space, emphasizing the interconnected nature of all living entities.

Cells and Genes: Epigenetics

Epigenetics is an intriguing and emerging area of scientific research that delves into the study of how cells control gene activity without altering the DNA sequence. Unlike traditional genetics, which solely focuses on the sequence of DNA building blocks, epigenetic changes are modifications attached to the DNA that determine whether genes are turned on or off. These modifications can effectively change the way our body reads a DNA sequence, influencing gene expression.

The term "epi-" in epigenetics comes from the Greek word meaning "on or above," emphasizing the layered nature of genetic control. Fascinatingly, research in this field has revealed that our behaviors and environment play a significant role in causing changes that impact our genes. Recent scientific findings have demonstrated that early experiences in childhood can profoundly determine gene expression, with the power to turn genes on and off. This groundbreaking research challenges the long-standing belief that genes are "set in stone,"

Dr. Bruce Lipton is not your average cell biologist, he's a trailblazer on a mission to unlock the secrets of our genes and how they interact with the environment. As a faculty member at the University of Wisconsin's School of Medicine and researcher at Stanford Medical School, Dr. Lipton made waves with his groundbreaking stem cell research and paved the way for the revolutionary field of epigenetics.

Back in the late 80s and early 90s, when terms like epigenetics were not yet in vogue, Dr. Lipton discovered that our environment has the power to turn our genes on or off through our cell membranes. This debunked the prevailing belief of genetic determinism, which claimed that our genes solely determined our traits from conception. But, of course, breaking through such entrenched beliefs wasn't easy, and Dr. Lipton faced resistance from the established scientific community.

Dr. Bruce Lipton's groundbreaking stem cell experiment revolutionized our understanding of genetics and the role of the environment in determining cell fate. By growing cells in a laboratory medium, similar to blood, he created three slightly different versions of this culture medium and placed them in separate Petri dishes. Genetically identical cells were then placed in each dish. The astonishing outcome was that the cells in one dish developed into muscle, those in another turned into bone, and those in the last dish became fat cells. The only difference between the dishes was the composition of the culture medium, highlighting the profound influence of the cellular environment on genetic activity.

This finding challenged the long-held belief that genes alone determine cell fate. Despite facing resistance from the medical establishment that clung to the deterministic view of genes, Lipton's experiment could not be disproven. It was only after two decades of persistence that the concept of epigenetics, which aligns with Lipton's findings, gained acceptance in the scientific community. Dr. Bruce Lipton was truly ahead of his time, shaking the foundations of traditional scientific thinking.

Lipton's experiment on stem cells is highly relevant to humans because, just like stem cells, we are comprised of countless cells that make up our body. It's like we are a gigantic petri dish covered in skin, with our blood serving as the culture medium that contains the information controlling our cells. While we are born with a specific combination of genes, we now understand that genes themselves do not make decisions.

So, where are our decisions being made? The answer lies in our brain. This incredible organ is responsible for deciding on the environment, or the culture medium, which is our blood. Our brain secretes neuropeptides, chemical messengers, into our bloodstream, thereby changing the environment.

By controlling the chemistry that is put into our blood through our thoughts and emotions, we have the power to influence our biology and shape our health. The mind, represented by the brain's perception of it, plays a crucial role in this process. It is the imagery that the brain is trying to complement with chemistry, translating the mind's image into neurochemicals, hormones, growth factors, and regulatory agents. These secretions then travel throughout our body, causing it to physically reflect the image in our mind. So, positive and negative thoughts can affect the gene environment and influence our overall well-being.

Contrary to popular belief, our health and the expression of diseases is not solely determined by our genes. In fact, genes are responsible for less than 1 percent of diseases. The remaining 99 percent is determined by how we respond to the world around us, which is heavily influenced by our mindset. This means that our conscious mind plays an instrumental role in our health outcomes. By practicing mindfulness and consciously controlling our emotions, we can live in a positive mindset and experience vibrant health. Positive emotions such as love and happiness trigger the release of dopamine and vasopressin, making us feel happier, more beautiful, and full of life. Conversely, negative emotions like fear and stress lead to the release of stress hormones and inflammatory agents, which can be detrimental to our well-being.

By understanding the mind-body connection, we can harness the power within us to heal and overcome illness. With a focused conscious mind, the brain can release the necessary chemistry into the blood to change the environment of our genes. This, in turn, allows for the modification or turning on and off of genes to address health issues, much like the placebo effect. By incorporating mind-body practices and embracing a positive mindset, we hold the key to unlocking our true potential for optimum health and vitality.

Connection to Manifestation

To connect this information to the concept of manifestation, it is important to consider the role of consciousness and intention in influencing our reality. If we consider the research, which suggests that cells possess a form of consciousness, we can hypothesize that our thoughts and intentions may also influence the cellular level of our being, potentially impacting our overall well being and ability to manifest.

Understanding manifestation requires recognizing that our thoughts and intentions are powerful forces that can shape our reality, it is possible that the cells within our bodies partake in this process of manifestation. If our cells possess consciousness and can communicate with each other, it is conceivable that they can also respond to our thoughts and intentions.

Dr. Bruce Lipton's theories about manifestation explore the power we have to change our environment and perceptions. He emphasizes that our belief systems play a crucial role in manifesting our desires and creating the life we want. Lipton explains that our conscious thoughts and subconscious mind form these belief systems, and it is not just our own thoughts that affect us, but also the thoughts and vibrations of those around us. Our thoughts and beliefs send out vibrations that influence not only our own lives but also the lives of others.

Lipton asserts that your conscious mind is creative and powerful, allowing us to imagine and manifest our desires and aspirations. However, the conscious mind can only work effectively if there are supporting programs in the subconscious mind. Research shows that our conscious minds only control about 5 percent of our cognitive behavior, while subconscious programs control a whopping 95 percent of our lives. This highlights the importance of addressing and reprogramming the subconscious source of limiting thoughts and beliefs. Doing so, we can empower ourselves and align our conscious desires with our subconscious patterns. This concept is central to Lipton's *new biology*, which emphasizes our role as creators of our own lives.

Deepak Chopra, one of the best known and prominent figures in alternative medicine, who has collaborated with Cleve Backster, expands upon these findings confirming that manifestation is a dance between our thoughts and the bio-communication abilities of our cells, choreographed by the universe.

Chopra argues that our thoughts and intentions can influence the electromagnetic activity in our cells. He believes that the cells in our bodies are not mere biological entities, but rather active participants in our conscious experience. When we focus our attention and energy on manifesting a desired outcome, it is possible that our conscious intent communicates with our cells, initiating a chain reaction that sets in motion the necessary processes for manifesting our desires.

Chapter 8

Consciousness: The Inner World

"The day science begins to study non-physical phenomena, it will make more progress in one decade than in all the previous centuries of its existence." - Nikola Tesla

Subconscious Mind: Abundance on Auto-Pilot

This is one of my favorite topics. When I learned about my subconscious mind and the Reticular Activating System (RAS), it really changed the way I looked at myself, my past, and my future. I feel like this is such a hidden secret that so many people know nothing about.

I really think this should be taught in school, probably high school, when our young people are beginning to shape who they are and thinking about who they will be and what they will become as adults in this world. I wish I had known about this topic earlier in my life. All I want to do now is tell as many people as I can about the power of the subconscious mind and how any of us can manipulate it.

What's more, science has known about this since the 1940s and since that time studies have expanded their depth of knowledge. Basically RAS is a bundle of nerves that sits in your brainstem and is responsible for sensation, consciousness, attention, and the sleep-wake cycle.

The RAS can be compared to a filter or a nightclub bouncer that works for your brain. It makes sure your brain doesn't have to deal with more information than it can handle. It can regulate the sensory information you perceive daily.

The part that fascinates me is that the RAS can take instructions from your conscious mind, passing them off to your subconscious. So you can shape your unconscious mind by overriding it, so to speak.

This is so amazing to me because the subconscious mind controls a huge percentage of our lives, and if you aren't aware of it, then you aren't going to realize that your mind can change your reality.

This is real science. You can change your reality. I will get into the specifics of RAS in a moment. But first let's look into how the science of our conscious and subconscious minds has evolved.

The Subconscious Mind: What we Know

"The subconscious mind is more powerful than the conscious mind. We must feed it positive, empowering thoughts to create the reality we desire." - Napoleon Hill

Your subconscious mind plays a powerful role in shaping your thoughts, actions, and ultimately, your reality. On average, 95 percent of brain activity is handled by the subconscious mind, leaving 5 percent of brain activity for our conscious minds. It acts as the control center of your mind, processing and storing vast amounts of information and influencing your everyday decisions. To understand how your subconscious mind steers you toward what it thinks about, we need to dive into the fascinating mechanisms at work within your mind.

Your subconscious mind operates on a series of interconnected processes. One of the most important is the Reticular Activating System (RAS), a network of neurons located in the brainstem. The RAS acts as a filter, constantly scanning and processing the sensory information your mind receives from the external world. It selectively amplifies certain inputs based on what it deems relevant and important to you.

Imagine searching for a new car. Suddenly, you start noticing the same car model everywhere, even though it wasn't something you paid much attention to before. This is the RAS in action. Once your subconscious mind registers something as significant, it starts directing your attention toward it. It's like having a personal assistant whose sole focus is to bring to your attention what you truly desire or believe to be important.

However, the RAS is not the only mechanism driving your subconscious mind's steering capabilities. It also heavily relies on your beliefs, values, and past experiences. Over time, your mind has formed a vast database of memories and associations that shape your view of the world. These stored memories create schemas, which are mental frameworks or blueprints that help your mind make sense of new information.

Let's say you have a belief that you are not capable of achieving abundance in your life. Your subconscious mind will generate thoughts and emotions aligned with that belief, steering you away from opportunities and limiting your actions. Conversely, if you hold a belief that abundance is attainable, your subconscious mind will actively seek out experiences and opportunities that align with that belief, steering you toward them.

It's important to note that your subconscious mind doesn't possess the ability to differentiate between positive and negative. It merely operates based on the information it has received and the beliefs it has formed. As a result, if you consistently focus on lack or limitations, your subconscious mind will interpret those as what you desire and steer you in that direction. It's like giving the wrong coordinates to a GPS system; you'll end up somewhere you didn't intend to be.

Let's say someone grew up in a household where money was always a struggle and they constantly heard phrases like "money doesn't grow on trees." As a result, their subconscious mind has formed a belief that abundance is scarce and difficult to attain. This belief will steer them away from opportunities for financial growth and success, as their subconscious mind will prioritize filtering out information that aligns with their belief in scarcity.

On the other hand, imagine someone who had supportive parents who encouraged them to pursue their dreams and believe in their abilities. Their subconscious mind has formed a belief that they are capable and deserving of success. As a result, their subconscious mind will actively seek out opportunities and experiences that align with their belief, steering them toward a path of accomplishment and abundance.

To steer your subconscious mind toward what you truly want, it is crucial to first identify and change any limiting beliefs or negative thought patterns. This requires conscious effort and the willingness to challenge and reframe old, unhelpful beliefs. By replacing them with positive and empowering beliefs, you are essentially recalibrating your subconscious mind's direction and opening up the pathway to manifesting abundance in your life.

Science at Work

There are a number of scientifically proven techniques that have emerged through innovative technology, giving scientists a glimpse into the mysteries of how our consciousness works inside our brains. This brief survey of various neuroimaging and computational advancement technology gives us a better picture of the various domains in our brain such as cognition and memory, along with behavior, emotion, and perception. And in turn, these studies shed light on the connection between them and our understanding of conscious and subconscious processes.

Transcranial magnetic stimulation (TMS) has been used to investigate the role of specific brain regions in motor function. By stimulating or disrupting targeted brain areas using magnetic fields, researchers can temporarily interfere with motor processes and observe the resulting changes in behavior. This helps establish causal relationships between brain activity and behavior, contributing to our understanding of conscious and subconscious motor control.

Researchers use functional magnetic resonance imaging (fMRI) to study the brain activity of individuals while they perform specific tasks. For example, they may ask participants to solve math problems while monitoring their brain activity using fMRI. This technology helps identify which areas of the brain are active during problem-solving, providing insights into the cognitive processes involved.

Electroencephalography (EEG) has been used to study the

sleep patterns of individuals. By placing electrodes on the scalp, researchers can monitor the electrical signals generated by the brain during sleep stages such as REM (rapid eye movement) and non-REM sleep. EEG helps identify patterns and changes in brain activity that correspond to different stages of sleep.

Magnetoencephalography (MEG) has been used to study the neural processes underlying visual perception. Using MEG, researchers measure the magnetic fields generated by visual stimuli presented to participants. By analyzing the MEG data, they can identify the specific brain regions involved in processing visual information, providing insights into the subconscious processes of visual perception.

Computational techniques and machine learning algorithms have been applied to fMRI data to identify patterns associated with different emotional states. Researchers collect fMRI data while participants experience different emotions, such as happiness, sadness, or fear. By analyzing the data using computational methods, they can develop models that accurately classify an individual's emotional state based on their brain activity. This demonstrates the potential for using computational approaches to understand conscious and subconscious emotional experiences.

fMRI has also been used to study memory processes. Participants may be asked to memorize and recall specific information while their brain activity is monitored using fMRI. By comparing brain activity during encoding and retrieval phases, researchers can identify the neural networks involved in memory formation and retrieval. This provides insights into the conscious and subconscious processes underlying memory.

Overall, these examples illustrate how neuroimaging technologies and computational advancements have accelerated our understanding of conscious and subconscious processes in various domains, such as cognition, emotion, perception, memory, and behavior.

The Search for Answers

Science has come a long way in understanding the human brain. We know that it is made up of an astounding 90 billion neurons, forming an intricate network of 100 trillion synaptic connections. This incredible organ regulates every aspect of our physical body's functioning, keeping us alive without us even having to think about it. However, when it comes to exploring our consciousness, science has fallen short.

The challenge lies in the fact that science requires evidence, something tangible to test and observe. But consciousness is intangible; you can't hold it, examine it, or see it. You can only hear it, and even then, only if it's your own. This creates a significant gap in the narrative of traditional science, leaving the mysteries of consciousness largely ignored for too long.

It's undeniable that there is a growing need for researchers to explore our consciousness and subconscious experience. Is consciousness solely a product of matter and biology, or is there something more profound at play? These burning questions demand our attention, as we search for the missing link that unlocks the secrets of our very existence.

In the pursuit of understanding consciousness, quantum physics has emerged as a fascinating avenue for exploration. Could the bizarre and counterintuitive principles of quantum mechanics shed light on the enigma of conscious experience? Perhaps the strange and interconnected nature of quantum interactions can help explain the complexities of our own minds.

The time has come for consciousness research to take center stage. We need to challenge ourselves to look deeper, to question the limitations of our current scientific framework, and to embrace the potential insights offered by quantum physics. By pushing the boundaries of conventional understanding, we can inch closer to unraveling the greatest mystery of all, the miracle of our own existence.

Sentience and Consciousness in Single Cells

There is a growing understanding among scientists that sentience, or awareness, may be present in all forms of life, including single cells. This idea challenges traditional views in evolutionary biology, which typically consider sentience to be a feature that emerged at a certain point in certain species. However, it is increasingly recognized that sentience is a necessity for adaptive life. While this perspective has been expressed by some biologists in the past, it has not been widely accepted as part of the standard model.

One reason for the resistance towards recognizing sentience in single cells is the lack of coherent mechanisms explaining how non-sentient molecules can give rise to conscious experiences. This concept, often referred to as the "hard problem" of consciousness, has been largely neglected by cell biologists.

However, in 2019, researchers Frantisek Baluska and Arthur Reber put forth a study that explored the emergence of sentience and consciousness in unicellular organisms. Their focus on single cells and the fundamental role of subjective awareness in cellular life highlights the need for an evolutionary theory that considers mechanisms occurring in prokaryotes, the simplest unicellular species.

The study explains the concept of sentience or consciousness in unicellular species as the presence of feelings, subjective states, and a primitive awareness of events, including internal states. These forms of sentience are likely experienced on a valenced continuum, with positive or negative states that influence actions.

For instance, when a prokaryote encounters a nutrient-rich environment, it experiences a feeling of satisfaction and may decide to suspend locomotion. Conversely, when faced with a high salt content, the prokaryote may experience a negative subjective state and move back towards a more favorable environment. In both cases, prokaryotes exhibit valence-marked, subjective, and internal states of awareness, which can be referred to as sentience or consciousness.

One of the reasons why there has been little research into the topic of sentience and consciousness in single cells can be attributed to the predominant focus on "human" consciousness. Historically, the scientific community has centered its exploration of consciousness on Homo sapiens, overlooking the possibility that consciousness may exist in other forms of life.

In fact, in 2005, the American Association for the Advancement of Science ranked the biological basis of consciousness as the second most important unsolved scientific problem, assuming it pertained solely to human consciousness. This anthropocentric approach has sparked vigorous debates within the field, and has hindered progress in understanding the origins and nature of consciousness.

The Baluska and Reber proposal revolutionizes our understanding of sentience and consciousness by suggesting that its origins lie in single cells. Unlike other theories that struggle to define the emergence of these cognitive functions, this proposal provides a tangible framework and directs our attention to the very beginning of life.

According to the study, the appearance of sentience, awareness, and consciousness occurred with the first emergence of life in single cells. These cells became the birthplace of the first minds, and all subsequent species inherited their mental states and functions from this event. This critical moment was unique and unparalleled on our planet, with every other species carrying genetic material that codes for sentience.

Just as all life followed a common evolutionary path, all forms of mental life, including the complexity of human consciousness, can be traced back to this single origin. This is a profound insight that emphasizes the interconnectedness of all living beings and underscores the fundamental importance of understanding the sentience and consciousness that resides within even the tiniest of cells.

Cognition-Based Evolution

In a 2021 study titled "Non-Random Genome Editing and Natural Cellular Engineering in Cognition-Based Evolution," researchers William B. Miller, Jr., Francisco J. Enguita, and Ana Lucia Leitao proposed the intriguing concept of Cognition-Based Evolution (CBE). This new theory also challenges the widely accepted notion of Neo-Darwinism, which posits that genetic variation occurs randomly and is subject to natural selection.

Instead, CBE suggests that biological variation is the result of intelligent cells collectively evaluating and responding to ambiguous environmental cues. These cells engage in non-random natural genomic editing in response to epigenetic impacts and environmental stresses.

According to this theory, cellular cognition is the foundation of biology and its evolutionary processes. Like the theory previously discussed, intelligent cells have the ability to receive, assess, communicate, and deploy information to maintain their self-integrity. CBE builds on this premise and extends the idea into the realm of evolution. Instead of relying solely on chance, CBE emphasizes that variation arises from cellular measurements, enabling collaborative ecological units across different cellular domains.

Cognition-Based Evolution presents a non-conventional framework for understanding the sources of evolutionary variation, asserting that intelligent cells utilize both random and non-random genetic variations to adapt and thrive in their environment.

The capacity for self awareness and intelligence does not exist solely in the minds of higher organisms with complex nervous systems, but can also be found in the fundamental unit of life itself: the cell. This concept emphasizes the importance of self-referential assessment in living entities, which separates them from machines or automata. It is through this sense of 'self' that biological development and immunological context are defined.

Cells possess the ability to measure their internal state as well as the external environment, and this information is abundantly communicated to other cells. Recent research has demonstrated that it is this cell communication that drives the interconnected tissue systems necessary for living forms to thrive.

Overall, this theory suggests that basal cognition, embodied in the cellular form, enables cellular sensorimotor functions and problem-solving through self-measurement and directed cell-to-cell communication. In this perspective, genes are seen as tools used by intelligent cells in their co-engineering process.

These intelligent measuring cells communicate with each other through a cellular information cycle, which is dictated by the principles of thermodynamics. Within this intricate network, cells measure and collaborate with each other in order to adapt and effectively respond to various environmental challenges. Hence, cellular engineering signifies the active manifestation of the cell's information management system.

This active information management allows cells to interact and cooperate in multicellular ecologies, where they work together to achieve collective goals and maintain organismal homeostasis. Through natural cellular engineering, cells harness their innate intelligence and adaptability to ensure the survival and success of the organism as a whole. It is as if these cells possess a deep-rooted understanding that their choices and actions play a pivotal role in the destiny of the species.

Cognition-based evolution sheds new light on the innate intelligence and problem-solving capabilities of cells, painting a picture of life as a grand tapestry of interconnected and purposeful microcosms striving for their own survival and collective progress.

Again in 2022, František Baluška, Arthur S. Reber, along with William B. Miller, Jr. expanded on the idea of single cell consciousness and evolution. Their new study discusses the biomolecular structures and processes that allow for and maintain this cellular consciousness from an evolutionary perspective in an article entitled "Cellular Sentience as the Primary Source of Biological Order and Evolution".

Thus the theory in Cognitive Based Evolution continues to be explored. Their model is based on the biomolecular mechanisms of cellular consciousness. Eukaryotic cells can be seen as "cells within cells," with organelles like mitochondria and plastids functioning as semi-autonomous endosymbiotic cells. The emerging idea of the symbiotic origin of the nucleus further challenges our understanding of cellular organization and opens up new avenues for exploration. Also cells possess their own electromagnetic fields, and are highly receptive to external electromagnetic fields.

This study offers support to the promising avenue for enhancing our understanding of cellular sentience as the primary driver of biological order and evolution.

Recent Research on Consciousness

One controversial view proposed by researchers Hameroff and Penrose is the concept of "quantum consciousness". They suggest that microtubules in neurons in the brain might temporarily maintain superposition states, exhibiting quantum properties.

Their work argues that the measurements of these superposition states in the brain make human conscious experience possible. This view has been met with skepticism and controversy, but it calls for further investigation to fully understand its implications.

I believe Dr. Danko D. Georgieva, serving as a visiting researcher at the renowned University of California, Los Angeles (UCLA), is on to something. His work spans across various disciplines, including quantum foundations, physics, chemistry, neuroscience, information science, and applied mathematics.

In one of his studies exploring consciousness, Georgieva delves into the mind-body problem using quantum information theory. This mind-body problem, which classical physics cannot solve, revolves around the challenge of explaining how the brain generates the unseen realm of conscious experiences.

In a captivating article published in May 2023, Georgieva delves further into the concept of consciousness and its causal influence in the physical world. Drawing from the notion that physics is the most fundamental scientific discipline encompassing all aspects of existence, Georgieva argues that consciousness should be defined as physical. By defining consciousness as non-physical, we sever its connection to physics and render it unable to have any causal effects on the physical world.

Incidentally, recent studies have also classified consciousness as a physical phenomenon, and Georgieva believes that quantum information theory can serve as a solid foundation for consciousness research, clarifying the distinction between the mind and the brain.

Our personal conscious minds undoubtedly exist. You know it, I know it, and science knows it. Therefore, if something exists science must classify it as a physical entity. Georgieva's focus is to identify existing physical theories or perhaps future physical theories that can encompass conscious experiences and their impact on the physical world.

In his article "Causal potency of consciousness in the physical world", Georgieva posits that the physical theory of quantum reductionism emphasizes the causal potency of the conscious mind and its ability to affect the physical world, giving credence to the idea that our minds can truly transform our surroundings.

Quantum mechanics already possesses the necessary mathematical ingredients to support a causally potent consciousness. This mind-brain theory suggests that our conscious mind can be identified with the quantum state of our brain. Through physical measurements and quantum stochastic dynamics, our unobservable mind is constructed.

The implication of quantum reductionism is clear: Our conscious mind possesses free will and the capacity to choose among future courses of action. This is made possible through the wave function collapse and disentanglement process, where one of the multiple outcomes is actualized.

This actualization process, referred to as wave function collapse, occurs when the quantum system reaches a certain energy threshold. By allowing for these actualizations and dynamic trajectories produced by sequential choices, quantum physics not only solves the measurement problem but also supports the causal potency of consciousness.

Understanding the role of quantum mechanics in our conscious choices and their effect on our physical reality is crucial. It highlights the transformative power of our minds and the potential for us to manifest our desired environment.

Quantum physics is not merely an extravagant theory but rather an essential framework that enables us to describe and comprehend the dynamic nature of our consciousness, namely, that our brains and consciousness are uniquely equipped to shape and manifest the world around us.

What all this Means for Manifestation

Recalibrating your Reticular Activating System (RAS) positions your subconscious mind to steer you toward the things that are important and relevant to you. When you begin to actively practice the art of manifesting, your desires will be programmed into your subconscious and the RAS will become an instrument in realizing your desires.

The 2019 research study that explored the emergence of sentience and consciousness in unicellular organisms correlates to the art of manifestation in a profound way. Because we are physical beings in this physical world, our physiology plays an important role. If every cell in our body has a subjective awareness of its own, and we are in control of our mind, then it stands to reason that we are also in control of our bodies, and thus, we are in control of all of our cells. With this knowledge, aligning our conscious desires with the consciousness of each of our cells, magnifies our manifestation powers. In effect, you are creating what you want in your life, with your powerful conscious will, along with every cell in your body.

The concept of "quantum consciousness" suggests that microtubules in neurons in the brain might temporarily maintain superposition states, exhibiting quantum properties. This theory proposes that the act of measurement (observation) of these superposition states in the brain make human conscious experience possible. This idea relates to manifestation as a part of our consciousness. When we consciously observe a desire in our minds, we can possibly tap into a superposition state that we want to manifest by utilizing the quantum properties of the limitless possibilities residing in the neurons in our brains.

As recently as 2023, Dr. Danko D. Georgieva, using quantum information theory, developed the idea about the causal potency of consciousness in the physical world. Using the physical theory of quantum reductionism, he emphasizes the causal potency of the conscious mind and its ability to affect the physical world, giving credence to the idea that our minds can truly transform our surroundings.

The conclusion of this study highlights the implication that our conscious mind possesses free will and the capacity to choose among future courses of action made possible through the wave function collapse and disentanglement process, where one of the multiple outcomes is actualized. Understanding the role of quantum mechanics in our conscious choices and their effect on our physical reality allows us to use the transformative power of our minds to manifest our desired outcomes.

As science aims to unravel the mysteries of consciousness, it is crucial to expand our thinking beyond the boundaries of conventional understanding and venture into the realms of quantum possibilities. The search for more answers will require innovative thinking, collaboration, and a willingness to embrace the unknown. With the right approach and continued scientific advancements, we may finally unravel the secrets that lie within our minds and bring a new level of understanding to our subconscious and conscious experiences.

JOURNAL AND WORKBOOK ACTIVITIES

1. In your journal make a list of your beliefs, values, and past experiences that might have influenced your RAS up until now.

2. Identify ones you'd like to alter or omit from your subconscious mind.

3. Create a list of affirmations you could use to re-program your subconscious brain.

4. Put these affirmations wherever you will see them most often.

5. Make a point of manifesting your new RAS "wish list" by meditating on the beliefs you want your subconscious mind to absorb.

EMPOWER

Manifestation Powers

In this section you will learn the basics needed to understand the Art of Manifestation. This knowledge is a continuation from the ideas presented in Section One. After learning the "how to" steps in the process of manifesting, each subsequent chapter will examine the underlying nuances that each element in the process possesses. It is imperative to empower yourself with the knowledge and science behind each impactful concept that all play a significant role in the sublime art of manifestation. This section reveals the secrets you need to create more abundance in your life and to manifest your wildest dreams in order to start living your best life now.

Chapter 9

DIY Manifestation: The "How To"

"Believe you can and you're halfway there." - Theodore Roosevelt

Do It Yourself, Your Way

There is no doubt that some people have a natural gift for manifesting their desires. They just seem to know how to make things happen without even thinking twice. I, myself, must admit that I have a little bit of that intuitive know-how within me. It's like a sixth sense that guides me towards my goals.

However, just because some are naturally gifted in manifesting, it doesn't mean the rest of us are left in the dark. The steps of manifestation have been widely accepted by most experts in the field. These steps have been tested and proven over time, and I believe they can work for anyone, including you. I wouldn't be sharing this knowledge with you if I didn't believe in its effectiveness. So, rest assured, you are in good hands.

As we dive deeper in this section of the book, I will explain each step in more detail in the chapters following it. But remember, there isn't a one-size-fits-all approach to manifestation. It's important to try different techniques and take what works best for you. What clicks for one person might not resonate with you, and that's perfectly fine. It's all about finding your own unique path towards manifestation success.

Belief is the cornerstone of effective manifestation. Doubts will sabotage your efforts, so it is imperative to firmly believe that your wish has already been granted. The fascinating thing is that the brain cannot differentiate between reality and imagination. This realization further emphasizes the power of maintaining positive emotions and an unwavering belief in the manifestation process.

Expressing gratitude acts as an accelerator in the manifestation journey. By cultivating gratitude for what you already have, you send out a powerful message to the universe that you are open to receiving more abundance. Additionally, consciousness meditation and being present in the now, play a significant role in manifesting your desires. These practices allow you to align your thoughts and emotions with your desired outcome, enhancing the manifestation process.

So, my friend, remember that there is no one way that is guaranteed to work for everyone. Find what resonates with you, embrace the belief that it is possible. Try everything! Try it again. Some may need more practice than others, but with unwavering belief and dedication, you too can tap into the power of manifestation and create the life you desire.

The Quantum Connection

Before you read the steps of "how to", you need to be reminded of how quantum physics ties in with manifesting, we must delve into the magical world of quantum mechanics to unravel the secrets of manifesting.

At the heart of quantum physics lies the principle that everything in the universe, including our thoughts and intentions, is made up of energy. As you should know by now, this idea is also supported by traditional science. But quantum physicists have long discovered that subatomic particles, such as electrons and photons, behave in strange and mysterious ways. They can exist in multiple places simultaneously, affect changes to their entangled partner particle instantaneously over vast distances, and their behavior is influenced by the mere act of observation.

But what does all of this have to do with manifesting our desires? It comes down to the concept of the observer effect and the interconnected nature of the universe. According to the observer effect, the very act of observing an event or phenomenon can influence its outcome. In other words, our thoughts and intentions have the power to shape our reality.

Quantum physics tells us that we are not separate from the world around us, but rather, we are intertwined in a vast field of energy. This field is often referred to as the quantum field, or the field of infinite possibilities. It is within this field that the manifestations of our desires can occur.

Just as subatomic particles can exist in multiple places at once, our desires also exist in this field as possibilities. When we harness the power of our thoughts and intentions, we can collapse these possibilities into specific outcomes, bringing our desires into physical reality.

Now, you might be wondering, how exactly does this process work? Well, it's all about the energy we emit. Our thoughts and intentions are not mere abstract concepts; they carry a certain frequency or vibrational energy. And just like tuning in to a specific radio station, we can tune in to the frequency of our desires through focused attention and intention.

When we align our thoughts and emotions with the frequency of what we want to manifest, we send out a powerful signal into the quantum field. This signal attracts and aligns with matching energies, ultimately bringing our desires into fruition. It is as if the universe conspires to bring together the necessary people, opportunities, and circumstances to make our desires a reality.

But it's not just about wishful thinking or positive affirmations. Quantum physics teaches us that to manifest our desires, we must truly believe, with absolute certainty, that what we desire is already ours. This belief is what physicists call the state of Quantum Superposition; the notion that particles can exist in multiple places or states simultaneously is a cornerstone of quantum physics. In other words, since there are limitless possibilities, we can choose the possibility of our desire and it will become a certain reality because we have observed it, recognized it, manifested it.

Quantum physics and the art of manifesting go hand in hand. By understanding and harnessing the underlying principles of quantum mechanics, we can tap into the vast field of infinite possibilities, shaping our reality and living our best lives now. The power to manifest abundance lies within us, waiting to be unlocked and unleashed. As you work through the steps below, don't forget to embrace the magic of quantum physics so you will be able to step into the realm of limitless potential.

How to Manifest, Step by Step!

1. Get clear on what you want. Start out simple with just one thing. The clearer you are about what you want, the easier it will be to manifest it. So take some time to sit down and really think about what it is that you want to bring into your life. Maybe you want to clear up your skin from blemishes, or have enough money to buy a new car. Whatever it is, be specific. Remember to be detailed. If you are new to manifesting, specific details are crucial.

2. Set your Intention. Your intention is a powerful way to manifest because it's what will guide your actions and help you stay focused on your goal. Take some time to sit down and really think about what it is that you want to achieve, whether it be to get a better job or go on a dream vacation. By making a conscious effort to set intentions, you will surely get closer to the life of your dreams.

3. Visualize what you want. When you do this, see yourself in a moment of time when what you want has already happened. Where are you? Who are you with? What are you doing? And the more vivid and realistic your visualization, the better. A great idea to keep this vision alive is to create a vision board and fill it with images of your desires, or to write down your visualization on a piece of paper or in your journal. Write it like a script for a movie, with characters, dialogue, and setting. Then as a novelist would do, describe what you see, hear, smell, taste or touch. What is the weather? What are the inner thoughts you are having in the scene? Explore how everyone in your visualization is feeling. This is the last scene of the movie, when you, the protagonist, have overcome every obstacle and are triumphing in the moment.

4. Focus on your Emotions. The next step is to focus on your feelings. While you are visualizing, feel the emotions of how you will feel when this desire comes to be. Meditate on these feelings for a good amount of time while you are visualizing. Feel so deeply, that you will remember the moment, this moment, of when you first really visualized your desire coming true. If you do this with conviction and truly dig deep to feel, you are, in essence, tricking your brain into thinking it has already happened. These true emotions that you conjure up, will be encoded in your body. Your body then, sort of becomes your mind. Your mind will feed off the body's emotions and believe that this has already happened.

5. Honor Gratitude. Right after you visualize and feel the emotions go straight into feeling grateful. Focus on as many parts of your life as you can, that you feel gratitude for. Picture these people, places, and things in your mind and let joy and gratitude fill you up with a white glowing light. Gratitude is the highest state of receiving and a powerful manifesting tool because it allows you to be able to receive. And you must be open to receiving and trust that the universe will bring you what you want. When you focus on the positive aspects of your life through gratitude, the more positive things will come into your life. Make keeping a daily gratitude journal a new habit. This will keep you in the right mindset and remind you of all the good things in your life!

6. Let go of your Attachment. After you've visualized with focused emotions and honored your gratitude, you are now finished with the first phase of manifesting. The next step is to let go. Do not get attached to the outcome. Even if you have a hard time letting go, it's important to do this in order to get what you want. You must surrender and detach yourself from

the expected outcome if you want the universe to bring you what you want. This shows the universe that you have faith and are open to receiving. If you don't truly let go of the outcome, your subconscious mind will know and it will sabotage all the effort you put into your visualization meditation.

7. Take Action. After you've done all of the above, take actionable steps. Actions let the universe know that you're serious about your goal. Manifestation isn't "magic" in the sense that you do nothing and something appears out of thin air. You need to make a plan. Think of any actions you can do to aid in your desired manifestation. It may be going places or being around people associated with your desire. It may be walking through a checklist of steps outlined in your plan. It can also be "living life" in the way it will be once your desire has manifested. As you move forward toward your goal, stay open and watch for signs and omens. Don't be surprised when you meet the right people or doors of opportunity are opened for you. Follow your gut and go with the flow of the universe that is leading you toward your desire. Taking actionable steps in whatever fashion, also helps you to stay focused and motivated, getting you closer to your goal.

8. Be Patient. Manifesting can sometimes take a while, so it's important to be patient and trust that all of nature wants to and will bring you what you want. Engage in positive things like doing random acts of kindness for others. Focus on positive daily affirmations. Maybe you do a different affirmation each day or each week, so that it becomes your north star. Be grateful for what is coming and what you already have. Believe with all your heart that what you want will happen. The universe may need time to put the pieces of the puzzle together, so as you flow with it know that everything that

happens is for a reason. Your trust and patience will allow the universe to let your desire manifest for you in the best way possible and at a time that is perfect for you.

9. Keep your Vibrations High. Your vibration is a reflection of your thoughts and feelings, so it's important to keep your energy frequencies positive if you want to attract big things into your life. Keeping your vibrations high will help in removing any negative thoughts that could arise. Wake up each morning knowing that this thing that you want is coming. Start every day with the joy of that knowledge and walk through each day with a happy countenance. Smile as much as you can, smiling is contagious and will raise your vibrations even if you're having a difficult moment or a tough day.

10. Do Not let Doubt Creep in. Doubt is the enemy and can sabotage all of your work. If a negative thought creeps in, crush it immediately. It is usually just mind chatter and isn't the real you, who has committed to manifesting what you want. Negative thoughts generated by your mind typically come up, so don't become frustrated. Just acknowledge it happened and then release the thought. Let go of any resistance you may feel from the conditioned matrix of your normal life. When a doubt comes up, literally tell your brain not to play that "thought movie" again. You are in charge. If you are strong in controlling which thoughts to linger on and which ones not to, the doubts and random negative suggestions will begin to diminish over time. Remember that you deserve this.

11. Trust the Process. Manifesting is a natural process, so it's important to trust that it will happen in its own time. You will be surprised when you see the power of manifestation come into your life in unexpected ways! When you have faith, you know that anything is possible and negative energy can be

banished from your life. My motto is DREAM BIG. BELIEVE. Use that! Miracles happen all the time.

12. Be Persistent. It is important to be persistent and never give up on your goal. Remember, the universe will bring you what you want, but it might take some time. You can continue to meditate and visualize your desire until it comes. However, it is a good idea to adjust the focus of your visualizations each time you do a manifestation meditation. Think quality, not quantity. One manifestation meditation done with absolute fidelity and sincerely felt emotions is really all you need. If you do more, change up the scene of your triumphant moment. This gives the universe more specifics about what you want. And remember, there may be a reason that you can't see now, about why one particular manifestation is taking longer than you expected. Be persistent, don't give up, stay positive, trust that nature wants you to have everything you desire, and keep taking action towards your goal.

JOURNAL AND WORKBOOK ACTIVITIES

In Chapter 11 there is a Manifestation Meditation you'll be able to use after you try it out on your own with the activities below.

In your journal identify all the areas in your life that you want to fill with abundance. In other words, make a list of all the things you want to manifest. Like a brainstorming session, write anything down that comes to mind. Examine every area of your life and let your imagination take hold. There is no reason why you can't have it all.

Choose one of the desires on your brainstormed list to start with. Pick something simple. In other words, it is better to start small and practice the "how to" steps for manifestation in this chapter. Do this as a visualization meditation. You will be so surprised when what you want happens! When you start small, it allows you to improve your skills over time.

Make a vision board and put it up where you can visit it each day. And/or write down your visualization scene in your journal.

Track your progress and constantly evaluate the skills you are building. You may mess things up: I know I did when I first started. If that happens, begin again or start fresh with a different desire. This is not failure, this is learning.

Chapter 10

The Meditation Revolution: Finding Your Zen

"Know well what leads you forward and what holds you back, and choose the path that leads to wisdom." - Buddha

Growing up, my Sundays were always filled with church services. It was a tradition that my family followed diligently, and I embraced it wholeheartedly. Prayer became an intrinsic part of my life, and I genuinely believed in its power. Every night, before going to bed, I would have personal conversations with God, pouring out my thoughts, concerns, and hopes. Prayer was my way of seeking help and guidance when faced with challenges.

As I grew older and started exploring different religions, I became fascinated whenever I heard about meditation. I dived into research, hoping to understand the practice better. Although I came across references to meditation in Judeo-Christian faiths, I rarely saw it being actively practiced within the communities I encountered. Despite my curiosity, meditation remained elusive in my life for many years. It wasn't until the past decade, when I found myself facing challenging circumstances and searching for answers within myself, that I truly began to understand meditation.

My journey led me to discover and experiment with different meditation techniques. I eagerly tried out numerous apps on my phone to deepen my practice and expand my knowledge. And oh, what a journey it has been! Each day, I learned more about the benefits and transformative power of meditation.

While I practice several different kinds of meditation depending on my needs, at present, I find myself drawn to consciousness meditation. It has become an integral part of my self-care routine, as I have realized its importance not only in manifesting my desires but also in enhancing overall well-being. Meditation provides a multitude of benefits, beyond aiding in the manifestation process. From stress reduction to improved focus and emotional well-being, it has truly transformed my life.

Whether you already practice meditation or are completely new to it, my aim in sharing this list is to provide you with an overview and a starting point on your own path of exploration. Meditation is a powerful tool that can bring about profound changes in your life. Embrace it as a vital aspect of your self-care practice, and let it guide you towards a more peaceful and fulfilling existence.

Some Meditation Practices to Consider

Below are just a few examples. There are many more types of meditation available. Each technique has its unique approach and purpose, catering to different individuals and their specific goals. Ultimately, it is important to explore different forms of meditation and find the one that resonates most with your preferences and objectives.

1. Consciousness Meditation: Often referred to as Mindfulness Meditation involves focusing one's attention on the present moment and observing thoughts and sensations without judgment by gently redirecting the mind back to the present when it wanders. It is commonly practiced by sitting in a comfortable position, focusing on the breath, stopping all your "doing" and just being in the "now", the present moment.

2. Transcendental Meditation: Transcendental Meditation is a technique where practitioners repeat a mantra silently to themselves, aiming to achieve a state of deep relaxation and inner peace. It is not associated with religion and was developed by Maharishi Mahesh Yogi. It is typically practiced for 20 minutes, twice a day, while seated with the eyes closed.

3. Metta Meditation: "Metta" means positive energy and kindness toward others. This form of meditation is also known as Loving Kindness Meditation, and involves cultivating feelings of love, compassion, and kindness towards oneself and others. Practitioners typically sit comfortably and mentally repeat loving-kindness phrases or send well wishes to others.

4. Zen Meditation: This is a form of seated meditation commonly associated with Zen Buddhism. It involves maintaining a certain posture (often the lotus or half-lotus position) while focusing on the breath or counting breaths. The goal is to develop insight and find the essence of one's true nature.

5. Vipassana Meditation: Vipassana, which means "insight" or "clear seeing," is a form of meditation taught in the Theravada Buddhist tradition. Practitioners often sit in a comfortable position and observe their bodily sensations, thoughts, and mental states without attachment or judgment. The aim is to develop insight into the impermanent and non-self nature of reality.

6. Kundalini Meditation: Kundalini Meditation involves various techniques, including deep breathing, chanting, and repetitive movements, to awaken the dormant spiritual energy believed to reside at the base of the spine. This practice aims to raise the Kundalini energy and achieve spiritual enlightenment.

7. Guided Visualization Meditation: In Guided Visualization Meditation, practitioners vividly imagine specific scenes, experiences, or journeys guided by a meditation teacher or audio recording. It often involves using multiple senses to enhance the visualization and deepen the meditative state.

8. Walking Meditation: Walking Meditation is a practice that combines mindfulness with the act of walking. Practitioners typically walk slowly and attentively, focusing on the sensation of each step, the breath, or the surrounding environment. It can be done indoors, in nature, or in a labyrinth.

9. Movement-based Meditation: Practices such as Tai Chi, Qigong, and walking meditation fall under this category. Movement-based Meditation involves cultivating mindfulness while engaging in slow, deliberate physical movements. Focus is directed towards the sensations and flow of movement, promoting a sense of calm and presence.

> *"To a mind that is still, the whole universe surrenders." - Lao Tzu*

Finding a Meditation for Me

Each type of meditation has its own unique benefits, so it's important to choose one that resonates with you and stick with it.

Jumping from one technique to another can prevent you from fully diving deep into the practice and experiencing its full benefits. Find a type of meditation that feels comfortable and natural to you, and give yourself the time and opportunity to fully explore it before moving on to the next.

Creating a calm and quiet environment for meditation is also crucial for optimal practice and results. Distractions, such as noisy environments or interruptions, can hinder your ability to fully concentrate and find the peace and stillness within. Find a quiet space where you can be alone and free from distractions. It could be a dedicated meditation space in your home, a peaceful spot in nature, or even just a quiet corner of a room where you can create a sense of serenity.

In order to see the best results, it's important to make meditation a daily habit. Set aside a specific time each day to practice, whether it's in the morning, during a lunch break, or in the evening before bed. By making meditation a regular part of your routine, you will reap the benefits and experience the positive effects on your mind and body.

These are just a few examples of the numerous forms of meditation available. The way people practice these techniques may vary depending on the specific type of meditation. However, it is crucial to note that no matter which form of meditation one chooses, consistency, commitment, and finding a calm and quiet environment free from distractions are essential for optimal practice and results.

JOURNAL AND WORKBOOK ACTIVITIES

Read through this checklist to help you evaluate and explore various meditation styles. Try them out and record your reactions and reflections in your journal.

1. Identify your goals: Consider what you hope to achieve through meditation, whether it be stress reduction, increased focus, emotional well-being, or spiritual growth.

2. Assess your preferences: Reflect on the type of meditation that aligns with your personal preferences and beliefs. Do you prefer a seated practice or something more active? Are you comfortable with guided instructions or do you prefer silence?

3. Consider your schedule: Determine how much time you can realistically dedicate to meditation each day. Some practices may require more time and commitment than others.

4. Research and learn: Familiarize yourself with the different forms of meditation mentioned in this chapter and any other types that may interest you. Learn about their techniques, benefits, and requirements.

5. Seek guidance: If possible, seek guidance from experienced practitioners or teachers in the form of classes, workshops, or online resources. They can provide valuable insights and support to help you get started and ensure proper technique.

6. Experiment and try it out: Start with one or two meditation practices that resonate with you the most. Try each one for a period of time to gauge how it feels and if it aligns with your goals and preferences.

7. Evaluate your experience: Assess the effectiveness and impact of each practice on your well-being. Consider factors

such as your ability to focus, the calmness of your mind, and the overall benefits you experience.

8. Make a decision: Based on your goals, preferences, schedule, guidance, and personal experience, choose a meditation practice that you feel suits you best.

9. Commit and establish a routine: Once you have made a decision, commit to practicing your chosen meditation regularly. Set aside dedicated time each day to establish a consistent routine.

10. Create a suitable environment: Ensure you have a calm and quiet space that is free from distractions to practice meditation. Set up any necessary props or items to facilitate your chosen practice.

11. Adapt and explore: As you continue practicing, remain open to exploring other forms of meditation that may complement or deepen your experience. Stay curious and receptive to new techniques and approaches.

12. Reflect and adjust: Regularly reflect on how your meditation practice is affecting your well-being and overall life. Make any necessary adjustments to your routine or practice as you progress on your meditation journey.

Remember, the ultimate goal is to find a meditation practice that resonates with you and supports your well-being. Trust your intuition and allow yourself to evolve and adapt as you deepen your understanding and experience of meditation.

Chapter 11

Sublime Transformation: Unleashing the Magic of Meditation

"Your thoughts become your reality." - Mahatma Gandhi

The Ultimate Tool

While some are able to manifest without engaging in meditation, I have found that meditation really is the ultimate tool, especially if you are trying to manifest a significant desire outside of the norms of your existing situation. But start small and work your way up. This will give you confidence and help you internalize the steps in the process.

Manifestation meditation is a powerful technique that combines the principles of mindfulness, visualization, and intention to create a desired outcome in one's life. This method is heavily influenced by the fields of neuroscience and quantum physics, and builds upon the idea that our thoughts and emotions have a direct impact on our reality.

To begin, it is important to understand that every thought and emotion we experience produces a corresponding chemical reaction in our body. These chemicals then influence our behavior and the way we interact with the world. By learning how to consciously direct our thoughts and emotions, we can alter these chemical reactions and thus change the way we experience our reality.

It is recommended to practice this technique on a daily basis, ideally in the morning or before going to bed, when the mind is more receptive to suggestions. By dedicating time and effort to this practice, you are actively reconditioning your mind and aligning yourself with the frequencies of your desired outcomes.

Various meditation techniques can be employed, such as mindfulness meditation, visualization, or mantra repetition, depending on personal preference and what resonates most with an individual. However, consistency and commitment to the practice are key in achieving desired results.

The Magic of Brainwaves

Brain waves are electrical impulses that continuously flow in your brain. There are four types of brain waves: Alpha, Beta, Delta, and Theta. Each one of these waves is associated with a distinct state of mind. The impact of brain waves on our bodies should not be underestimated. These waves have a profound influence on various aspects of our well-being, from our mood and emotions to our ability to sleep. Interestingly, brain waves not only impact our physical and mental states but also influence our cognitive abilities and internal thought processes.

Beta brain waves are best used when we are awake, active and alert. Beta waves occur during tasks that require concentration, problem-solving, and decision-making. Interestingly, beta waves are spontaneously present during REM (Rapid Eye Movement) sleep, which is when you dream. So, when you're dreaming, your brain is actually in an active and engaged state, which I find fascinating.

On the other end of the spectrum, we have Delta brain waves, which occupy the slowest frequency band. These brain waves occur during deep sleep and are associated with physical healing. It's during this deep sleep phase that our immune system is improved, and our stress levels are reduced. Delta brain waves are crucial for our overall well-being and help with tissue repair and regeneration.

Alpha waves are present during our sleep and awake stages. When we are awake, they promote a sense of mental readiness as we begin our day. They help us achieve a state of relaxation and calmness. When it is time for bed, we want to activate alpha waves so we can transfer more easily to sleep. They are also present in the first stage of sleep. Alpha waves improve our capacity to focus and concentrate. They have a positive effect on our overall mental well-being, as they reduce stress and anxiety.

Theta brain waves occur during the second phase of sleep, as deep sleep settles in. As we come out of sleep in the morning they are present. Theta activity can occur when you are awake and focused on your internal world, like when you are doing pure consciousness meditation. It is often associated with a relaxed, drowsy, or daydreaming state. Many describe the experience of theta brain waves as blissful and associated with positive emotions.

Theta waves are also associated with implicit learning, where we subconsciously pick up on information without deliberate attention. These waves are connected to a state of mental creativity where our imagination and intuition are heightened.

Meditating or engaging in activities like visualization can stimulate alpha and theta brain waves, facilitating relaxation and intuition. This is why it is recommended to practice meditation right before falling asleep or just after waking up, when we still are operating from our theta or alpha brainwave state.

It is worth noting that consistency and dedication are key when practicing manifestation meditation. It is recommended to incorporate this practice into your daily routine, setting aside dedicated time for meditation and visualization. By following this method with precision and commitment, women can tap into their innate power to create abundance and manifest their desires into reality.

The subconscious plays a significant role in manifesting desires, as it stores deeply ingrained beliefs, experiences, and programming that influence one's thoughts and actions on a subconscious level. In order to manifest abundance and overcome any limiting beliefs or self-sabotaging patterns, it is crucial to address and reprogram the subconscious mind through regular meditation practice.

I

JOURNAL AND WORKBOOK ACTIVITIES

1. Decide on something to manifest and set clear and specific intentions. This involves clearly defining what you want to manifest in your life. Whether it's a specific goal, a desired outcome, or a state of being, it is important to be as specific as possible. By doing so, you are providing your brain with a clear target to focus its energy and attention on.

2. Make sure to note the date when you do a manifestation meditation. In your journal each day, write down anything significant that comes into being that is in alignment with your specific desire. This might be in the form of coincidences, gut feelings, and hunches. It might be meeting the right people, being in the right place at the right time, and/or an increase of general "luck" being on your side.

3. You should record yourself and create your own guided meditation using the Basic Meditation for Manifestation Script below. Speak slowly and softly to yourself, and be encouraging and positive when you are reading the script.

4. Leave moments of silence after each paragraph in the script while you are recording, so you will have the time to fully engage with each guided step in your mind.

5. Find a recording of any Solfeggio Frequency to play in the background while you are recording your voice. I used a frequency at 741 Hz and played these musical tones while I recorded my first guided meditation.

6. After using a basic guided manifestation meditation, like the one that I first used, you will soon figure out how to do the meditation on your own. Ultimately you will find an optimal

way of doing a manifestation meditation and of course you should do what works best for you.

Basic Meditation for Manifestation Script:

"This is the now. Close your eyes and begin to focus your attention inward. This is the now. Take several deep breaths, in and out. Feel the rush of energy coming into your body as you breathe in and the release of oxygen as you breathe out, leaving you calm and centered."

"Now, release control of your breathing and allow it to become slow, deep, and rhythmic. In this state of heightened awareness you are quieting the chattering mind and entering into a state of stillness. This is the now. In this state, you create a space where new possibilities can take root."

"Begin to sense the energy inside your body. The space that your body occupies is part of the vastness of all the space that exists. Feel yourself, your body in this vast space of all that is."

"And now, can you become aware of the space between your body and the walls of the room? All the energy in the space around you is part of the space of this universe. This energy extends outward to all of space. Can you sense the volume of space that the entire room occupies?"

"And now, can you become aware of the space that all space occupies? Can you begin to sense the energy of everything in space? Become aware of all the space that space takes up."

"And it's time for you to become nobody, no one, no thing, no where, and in no time. It's time for you to become pure consciousness. This is the now. You must become aware of the infinite field of potential. You must invest your energy into the unknown. The longer you linger here in the unknown, the more you draw a new life towards you."

"Simply become a thought in the blackness of infinity. Unfold your attention into *no thing*, into *no body*, into *no time*. If you as the quantum observer find your mind returning to the known, to the familiar, to people, to things, or places in your familiar physical reality, to your body, to your identity, to the past and to past emotions, or to the predictable future, simply become aware that when your mind wanders, you are observing the known."

"Surrender your consciousness back into the void of possibilities so you can become *no one, no body, no thing, no where, in no time*. Unfold into the immaterial realm of quantum potentials. The more you become awareness and possibility the more you can create possibility and opportunity in your life. Stay present. Linger here. Pure consciousness. Invest your energy into the unknown."

*Wait in silence for a few minutes here, so you have time to fully be in the present moment.

"This is the now. I want you to make a decision with such firm intention, that the amplitude of that decision carries a level of energy that's greater than the hard wired programs in your brain and the emotional addictions in your body. Bring to your mind the desire you want to manifest. This decision needs your full attention and belief."

"Visualize yourself already experiencing the desired outcome of your decision. In this future moment, vividly imagine the scene of where you are, who you are with, what you are doing, and what is being said. Create a movie in your mind."

"Make it vivid and detailed, engaging all your senses to make the experience as real and powerful as possible. You are essentially "living" this reality in your mind. You are activating the same neural networks as if it were their reality in the present moment. You are rewiring your brain and creating new neural connections that support the desire you are manifesting."

"As you watch this scene play out over and over in your mind, you must also feel the emotions associated with it. Dig deep and feel the gratitude, joy, and love present in this mental rehearsal. Your strong feelings of emotions are sending clear and powerful coherent electromagnetic signals to the quantum field. Your body is absorbing your powerful emotions and will store them in your subconscious, enhancing your ability to attract the desired circumstances into your life."

"Allow your body to respond to a new mind. And allow this choice to become an experience that you'll never forget. And let the experience produce an emotion with such energy that it rewrites the programs and changes your biology. Continue to visualize for a few moments in silence."

*Wait in silence for a few minutes here, so you have time to fully perform your visualization.

"Now that you have visualized the future moment when your desire was made manifest, you must let go of any attachment to the outcome. Trust that the intention has been set in motion, and release any expectations or doubts. Allow the manifestation process to unfold naturally, without resistance or interference."

"Now you have changed your energy, so that your biology is altered by your own energy. Now it is time to surrender the past back into possibility and to allow the infinite field of possibilities to resolve in a way that's right for you. So give it up."

"It's time to move into a new state of being and allow your body to respond to a new mind. Change your energy by combining your clear intention with elevated emotion so that matter is lifted. Let this choice carry an amplitude of energy that's greater than any experience of the past. Let your body be altered by your consciousness using your own energy."

"Shift now into a new state of being. This moment defines you. Let your intentional thought become a powerful internal experience that carries an elevated emotional energy, which becomes a memory that you'll never forget."

"Be inspired. Become empowered. Make the choice through this decision that you will never fail to remember. Give your body a taste of the future by showing it how it will feel to believe this way. Let your body respond to a new mind. Open your heart and believe in possibility. Be lifted. Fall in love with the moment and experience that future."

"Now surrender that experience to a greater mind, for what you think and experience in this realm of possibility, if it is truly felt, it will manifest in some future time. From waves of possibility to particles in your physical reality."

"Don't forget, you are loved. You are energy. And you are connected to the Divine Intelligence. And you will flow through your day with ease because everything you need will come to you. Have a beautiful day. I love you."

Chapter 12

The Surprise Inside: How Emotions Shape Your Manifestation Power

"The greatest discovery of all time is that a person can change his future by merely changing his attitude." - Oprah Winfrey

A Few Words about Attitude

I think I'm gonna listen when Oprah Winfrey is quoted and gives us some hints about manifestation from her many inspirational quotes. She is without a doubt an extremely powerful manifester, she'll tell you that herself. She was born poor in rural Mississippi, to a soldier and an unwed teenage mother. Her childhood was tough by any standard but at 19, she became the first female African American news anchor in Nashville. And ultimately and incredibly, Oprah Winfrey used manifesting to become one of the world's wealthiest women.

I believe that in the beginning, when she started out, her positive attitude was the starting point in developing her powerful manifesting abilities. Studies show that having a positive outlook pays off. One study found that when compared to pessimists, *Visionary Work Optimists*, people in the top 25 percent for optimism as compared to their peers, are 40 percent more likely to get a promotion over the next year and six times more likely to be highly engaged at work.

These visionary work optimists may not have manifested their promotions but simply believed they had influence over their potential promotion and thus did the work that put them ahead. A positive attitude can do this. Looking at the glass half full or looking on the bright side has its benefits.

Another study shows that optimists spend less effort job searching and are offered jobs more quickly compared to pessimists. Yet another study shows optimistic people work harder, are more likely to remarry if they've divorced, and save more money.

Research shows that positive and optimistic people attract others. And the more people believe in you and your cause, the more chances you have to turn your crazy big dreams into reality. If you cultivate a positive attitude, a mindset of hope and opportunity, you will be vibrating with positive energy. You will see the world as a place of opportunity and not pain. The attitude you choose to live by is a key component in understanding your impact and shapes the direction of your life.

> *"Be thankful for what you have; you'll end up having more. If you concentrate on what you don't have, you will never, ever have enough.".- Oprah Winfrey*

You are in Control

It's a scientific fact that emotions precede thought. When emotions run high, they change the way our brains function, diminishing our cognitive abilities, decision-making powers, and even interpersonal skills. Managing and understanding our emotions helps us to be more successful in both our personal and professional lives.

The bottom line is: You're the one who gets to control your emotions, so they don't control you. Emotional Intelligence (EI) is a concept that defines one's ability to recognize, understand and manage our own emotions and along with recognizing, understanding and influencing the emotions of others.

In practical terms, this means being aware that emotions can drive our behavior and impact people, positively and negatively, and learning how to manage those emotions. There are twelve competencies of emotional intelligence namely: emotional self-awareness, emotional self-control, adaptability, achievement orientation, positive outlook, empathy, organizational awareness, influence, coaching and mentoring, conflict management, teamwork, and inspirational leadership.

It's not surprising to me that research has shown that women often score higher on emotional intelligence or empathy tests than men. Having low EI means that a person has difficulty recognizing and understanding their emotions and those of others. People with low EI may also have poor emotion regulation and find it difficult to use their emotions to attain personal goals.

If you feel like this is an area you may need to examine, there are several self tests online. To kick start developing your emotional intelligence begin with your consciousness, compassion, and your ability to create social and interpersonal connections.

To improve emotional intelligence you will need to be more self-aware. Being aware of your emotions and emotional responses to those around you can greatly improve your emotional intelligence. Learn to recognize how others feel and practice active listening. Communicate clearly and stay positive (there it is again). Finally, be open-minded, empathize, and listen to the feedback of others.

Understanding the power of positive thinking and recognizing that you are in control of your emotions, will set you up for success, when using the power of your emotions to control your manifestation powers.

Emotional Power

The exploration of the connection between emotions and manifestation offers valuable insights into how our thoughts and feelings shape our reality. Emotions play a critical role in the process of manifesting better health and abundance in our lives.

Emotions are created by the chemicals that are released in our bodies in response to our thoughts and beliefs. These chemicals, known as neuropeptides, are essentially the messengers that communicate with our cells, influencing their behavior and ultimately shaping our experiences. Therefore, the nature and intensity of our emotions directly impact the signals we send to our cells, which in turn affect the outcomes we manifest in our lives.

Emotions are the fuel that drives our intentions and connects us to the quantum field of infinite possibilities. We live in a universe governed by quantum physics, which reveals that everything is made up of energy and information. Our thoughts and intentions are forms of energy that interact with this energetic field, influencing the reality we experience.

When we experience positive emotions such as joy, gratitude, and love, our bodies release beneficial chemicals such as oxytocin and dopamine. These chemicals not only make us feel good, but they also send signals that promote health, well-being, and attract positive experiences into our lives.

Emotions generate strong electromagnetic signals that carry a specific vibrational frequency, and this frequency is what determines our resonance with the quantum field. When we experience positive emotions it is easier to attract our desires.

Conversely, negative emotions such as fear, doubt, and frustration lower our vibrational frequency, blocking our connection to the quantum field and impeding manifestation. When we allow negative emotions to dominate our thoughts and actions, we attract more of the same negativity into our lives. Negative emotions, especially anxiety and stress, trigger the release of hormones such as cortisol, which can disrupt the body's natural balance and impede the manifestation process.

When the Body Becomes the Mind

In order for manifestation to work for you, I must emphasize the importance of feeling the emotions associated with the desired outcome as if it has already come to be. This is because our emotions create a state of coherence between our thoughts and feelings, aligning our intentions with the energy of what we want to manifest.

Our emotions are connected to our bodies. Think about a time when someone suddenly contacted you with some kind of unsettling information. Maybe it was, "A dog just got hit by a car and I think it's yours" or "The boss wants to see you in his office, they've already fired half the staff this morning".

When we get alarming news like this, what happens? Why, your stomach drops of course. You feel a sudden pang of worry, a sudden dread that leaves you feeling weak or queasy. Feeling a lump in your throat, as tears well up in your eyes is another example, caused by strong emotions of sadness.

In essence, your body is your unconscious mind. It feels deeply. Which is why a broken heart is so painful and hurts so badly.

Feelings and emotions are the end product of past experiences. We remember things because we remember how they feel. When we remember trauma, loss, or betrayal, our brains release the same chemicals from that original moment and we actually relive it as we remember it.

I've given you all the steps for manifestation and they are all a part of the process. However, the step of feeling your emotions is key! After you have told the universe what you want and you are vividly visualizing yourself there in that future moment, when your manifestation has already come true, you must find it within yourself to actually feel with conviction the emotions in your body.

Why? Because in this step you are teaching your body what it will feel like emotionally BEFORE your desire is made manifest. If you do this correctly, your body, just like your mind, won't know the difference between what is real and what you have imagined.

And since your body is a huge part of your subconscious mind, this visualized experience along with your strong emotional feelings will become encoded in your subconscious. It will become a natural part of your future manifestation experience and your subconscious mind will steer the actions and interactions of your life toward making your manifestation happen, so as to be able to experience that same emotional feeling that you put so much emotional expression onto.

Every gene in your body will be expecting the outcome of your desired manifestation. This is because the environment signals the genes. And the end product of an experience in the environment is an emotion. It is all connected!

During this step of manifestation what you are actually doing is manipulating the biological functions in your body. When you begin to embrace the elevated emotions of your desire before it happens, you are signaling the genes AHEAD of the actual environment—the environment you will be in when what you want to happen actually happens.

Genes make proteins. Proteins are responsible for structure and function in your body. The expression of proteins is the expression of your life.

When we are doing the steps of manifestation, we must put the utmost importance into feeling emotions deep down into the core of our body and soul. We must create elevated emotions and teach our bodies what the future will feel like. This way your body will start to live in that future reality before it is manifested.

It is not enough to simply think positive thoughts; we must truly feel the emotions in our body to generate the corresponding chemical signals. By consciously choosing and cultivating the most positive and heartfelt emotions, we can influence the neuropeptides released in our bodies and thereby increase the probability of manifesting our desired outcomes.

By adopting specific practices to rewire our neural pathways and consistently experiencing positive emotions associated with our desires, we can enhance our ability to manifest the life we truly desire.

Happy Hormones

Get in touch with your good chemicals:

Dopamine: Known as the "feel-good" hormone, dopamine is a neurotransmitter that's an important part of your brain's reward system. It's associated with pleasurable sensations, along with learning, memory, and more.

Serotonin: This hormone and neurotransmitter helps regulate your mood, along with your sleep, appetite, digestion, learning ability, and memory.

Oxytocin: Often called the "love hormone," oxytocin is essential for childbirth, breastfeeding, and strong parent-child bonding. It can also help promote trust, empathy, and bonding in relationships. Levels generally increase with physical affection.

Endorphins: These hormones are your body's natural pain reliever, which your body produces in response to stress or discomfort. Levels may also increase when you engage in reward-producing activities such as eating, working out, or having sex.

JOURNAL AND WORKBOOK ACTIVITIES

Choose something you want to make manifest. In your journal write a scene, just like you'd see in a movie, about yourself after what you desire has been made manifest. With vivid detail explain where you are, who you are with, what you are doing and saying. Describe all the emotions that you are experiencing. Map out this scene and re-read it often so you can bring yourself to this future time when you are the most thrilled, overwhelmed with emotion, exhilarated, excited, joyful, proud, grateful and happy.

Consider engaging in activities that activate your good chemicals. Copy these activities into your journal and challenge yourself to do at least one activity a day.

1. Exercise
2. Partaking in activities that leave a smile on your face
3. Exposure to sunlight
4. Eating dark chocolate
5. Playing with pets
6. Listening to music
7. Hugging loved ones
8. Dancing
9. Laughing
10. Acupuncture
11. Massage
12. Smelling lavender
13. Having sex

Chapter 13

The Gratitude Effect: Amplified Manifestation Power

*"Wear gratitude like a cloak and it will feed
every corner of your life." - Rumi*

Gratitude Research

Gratitude, my dear readers, is not a mere virtue or a passing trend. It is a potent catalyst in the manifestation process, an essential tool that empowers us all. Allow me to share with you the profound role that gratitude plays on our journey towards achieving our desires and dreams.

Over the past five decades, numerous universities and organizations have delved into researching gratitude and its impact on personal growth, well-being, lifespan, and manifestation. This extensive body of research has provided valuable insights into the transformative power of gratitude in various aspects of life.

Take a look at some of the organizations and universities that have contributed to this field of study and some key findings from their research.

1. University of California, Davis: One noteworthy institution that has extensively researched gratitude is the University of California, Davis. Through multiple studies, researchers at UC Davis have revealed that regularly practicing gratitude results in reduced stress levels, improved sleep quality, and increased feelings of happiness and life satisfaction. They found that individuals who actively cultivated gratitude experienced stronger social connections and a greater sense of purpose in life. The study also demonstrated that individuals who actively practiced gratitude experienced higher levels of optimism, vitality, and overall well-being.

2. University of Pennsylvania: Another prominent research institution that has played a significant role in the study of gratitude is the University of Pennsylvania. Researchers at the Positive Psychology Center of UPenn have conducted numerous studies confirming the positive impact of gratitude on mental health and well-being. Their findings indicate that expressing gratitude regularly can increase positive emotions, improve relationships, and enhance overall psychological resilience.

3. Harvard University: This esteemed institution renowned for its research efforts, has also contributed to the field of gratitude research. Through their studies, Harvard researchers have discovered that cultivating gratitude leads to increased happiness, well-being, and overall life satisfaction. Moreover, individuals who practice gratitude regularly have been found to be more resilient and better able to handle challenges. They found that individuals who frequently practice gratitude experience reduced risk of heart disease, lower blood pressure, reduced symptoms of chronic pain, and a strengthened

immune system. These findings suggest that gratitude not only positively influences mental well-being but also has tangible benefits for physical health.

4. Greater Good Science Center: Based at the University of California, Berkeley, their studies have shown that gratitude interventions lead to increased resilience and decreased symptoms of depression and anxiety. Moreover, they found that gratitude practices can enhance prosocial behavior, empathy, and compassion, fostering more meaningful and fulfilling relationships. UC Berkeley found that people who regularly practice gratitude experience higher levels of happiness, vitality, and overall well-being. These individuals were also found to have lower levels of depression and stress, indicating that gratitude can improve our mental and emotional state.

These are just a few examples of the numerous organizations and esteemed universities that have researched gratitude extensively. The collective findings reveal that gratitude is a powerful tool for personal growth, happiness, and overall well-being. Incorporating gratitude practices into daily life can lead to improved mental health, stronger relationships, increased resilience, and enhanced physical health.

The benefits of gratitude can be split into five groups:
- Emotional benefits
- Social benefits
- Personality benefits
- Career benefits
- Health benefits

Gratitude and Emotional Benefits

Evidence shows that a regular attitude of gratitude can make us happier. Simply journaling for five minutes a day about what we are grateful for can enhance our long-term happiness by over 10 percent. (Emmons & McCullough, 2003; Seligman, Steen, Park, & Peterson, 2005). It also increases psychological well-being. Researcher Chih-Che Lin (2017) found a high level of gratitude has a strong positive impact on psychological well-being, self-esteem, and depression.

Gratitude enhances our positive emotions. Research has shown that gratitude reduces envy, facilitates positive emotions, and makes us more resilient (Amin, 2014). It also increases our self-esteem. Participants who completed a four-week gratitude contemplation program reported greater life satisfaction and self-esteem than control group participants (Rash, Matsuba, & Prkachin, 2011).

It should be no surprise then, that gratitude can help keep suicidal thoughts and attempts at bay. A study on the effects of gratitude on depression, coping, and suicide showed that grati-tude is a protective factor when it comes to suicidal ideation in stressed and depressed individuals (Krysinska, Lester, Lyke, & Corveleyn, 2015).

Gratitude and Social Benefits

Those who are more grateful have access to a wider social network, more friends, and better relationships on average (Amin, 2014). Those who communicate their gratitude to their friends are more likely to work through problems and concerns with their friends and have a more positive perception of their friends (Lambert & Fincham, 2011). It can also improve our romantic relationships. A recent study found evidence that expressing gratitude to our significant others results in improved quality in the relationship (Algoe, Fredrickson, & Gable, 2013).

Gratitude increases social support. One study showed that those who are more grateful have access to more social support. It reported that higher gratitude also leads to lower levels of stress and depression (Wood, Maltby, Gillett, Linley, & Joseph, 2008). Additionally, it can strengthen family relationships in times of stress. Gratitude has been found to protect children of ill parents from anxiety and depression, acting as a buffer against the internalization of symptoms (Stoeckel, Weissbrod, & Ahrens, 2015).

Gratitude and Personality Benefits

Gratitude can make us more optimistic. Regular gratitude journaling has been shown to result in 5 to 15 percent increases in optimism (Amin, 2014). A study on the effects of gratitude on positive affectivity and optimism found that a gratitude intervention resulted in greater tendencies towards positivity and an expanded capacity for happiness and optimism (Lashani, Shaeiri, Asghari-Moghadam, & Golzari, 2012).

With gratitude we become more spiritual. The more spiritual you are, the more likely you are to be grateful, and vice versa (Urgesi, Aglioti, Skrap, & Fabbro, 2010). Gratitude also makes us more giving. Evidence has shown that promoting gratitude in participants makes them more likely to share with others, even at the expense of themselves, and even if the receiver was a stranger (DeSteno, Bartlett, Baumann, Williams, & Dickens, 2010). Those who are grateful and less materialistic enjoy greater life satisfaction (Tsang, Carpenter, Roberts, Frisch, & Carlisle, 2014).

Gratitude and Career Benefits

In the workplace, gratitude can make us more effective managers. Gratitude research has shown that practicing gratitude enhances your managerial skills, enhancing your praise-giving and motivating abilities as a mentor and guide to the employees you manage (Stone & Stone, 1983). Those that are more grateful than others are also less likely to be impatient during economic decision-making, leading to better decisions and less pressure from the desire for short-term gratification (DeSteno, Li, Dickens, & Lerner, 2014).

Gratitude is an important factor in helping people find meaning in their job. It helps us to exhibit and apply our gifts and talents or strengths in our employment environments. It creates positive emotions and hope, and can assist you in finding your calling. (Dik, Duffy, Allan, O'Donnell, Shim, & Steger, 2015). Research has found that gratitude and respect in the workplace can help employees feel embedded in their organization, or welcomed and valued (Ng, 2016).

In a rigorous examination of the effects of gratitude on stress and depressive symptoms in hospital staff, researchers learned that the participants randomly assigned to the gratitude group reported fewer depressive symptoms and stress (Cheng, Tsui, & Lam, 2015).

Gratitude and Physical Health

A study on gratitude visits showed that participants experienced a

35 percent reduction in depressive symptoms for several weeks, while those practicing gratitude journaling reported a similar reduction in depressive symptoms for as long as the journaling continued (Seligman et al., 2005). It can also help to improve your sleep. A two-week gratitude intervention increased sleep quality and reduced blood pressure in participants, leading to enhanced well-being (Jackowska, Brown, Ronaldson, & Steptoe, 2016).

Remarkably, gratitude can reduce your blood pressure. Patients with hypertension who practiced gratitude at least once a week experienced a significant decrease in blood pressure, resulting in better overall health (Shipon, 1977). It can also increase your frequency of exercise. Study participants who practiced gratitude regularly for 11 weeks were more likely to exercise than those in the control group (Emmons & McCullough, 2003). Basically, gratitude can improve your overall physical health. Evidence shows that the more grateful a person is the more likely he or she is to enjoy better physical health, as well as psychological health (Hill, Allemand, & Roberts, 2013).

The abundance of research conducted by these research studies emphasizes the life-changing potential of gratitude. By embracing and cultivating gratitude, we can tap into a wellspring of positivity, unlock our full potential, and create a life filled with joy, purpose, and success.

Using Gratitude to Manifest

In the manifestation process, it is important to make practicing gratitude a daily habit and to be specific about what you are grateful for. I have a rule that I live by that helps me ensure my gratitude practice is consistent. Upon waking, I do not lift my head until I have identified three things I am grateful for.

If you are able to incorporate my morning gratitude habit into your life, you will soon find that coming up with fresh new ideas can stall your progress. So, when you first begin this magical practice, instead of calling up the most common and generic feelings of gratitude that we all have, such as being grateful for our loved ones and families, our health, or the roof over our heads, your focus should be specific.

For example, when expressing gratitude for your dog, think of an emotional moment you have recently experienced with your beloved pet. Be grateful for the small moment last week when you stubbed your toe on the coffee table, sat down on the couch in pain, and your dog came over to you and nuzzled his nose against you as if he knew you needed a little empathy. Remembering these small moments in your life and being grateful for them is much more powerful.

While still lying in bed, I typically review the events of the prior day and search my soul for small moments of my ordinary life that I can be grateful for. When I come up with one I let my mind remember that moment of gratitude, and I watch the movie in my mind, visually reliving it and most importantly, remembering how it made me feel. I sit with that moment in silence and let the emotions fill my heart with joy.

When we express gratitude, we shift our focus from lack and scarcity to abundance and possibility. We align ourselves with the energy of gratitude, an energy that is magnetic and attracts more of what we appreciate into our lives.

As we cultivate an attitude of gratitude, our thoughts, emotions, and actions become harmoniously aligned with our desires, amplifying our ability to manifest them.

Furthermore, gratitude acts as a powerful antidote to negative emotions that hinder our manifestation efforts. By acknowledging and appreciating the blessings and gifts we already have, we raise our vibrations and elevate our emotional state.

This positive shift enables us to let go of limiting beliefs, doubts, and fears, creating room for manifestation to thrive. Gratitude, you see, is not contingent upon the manifestation of our desires; it is a state of being that should permeate our lives.

Gratitude is an incredibly powerful tool in the manifestation process, as it acts as a magnet for attracting abundance and creating a positive mindset. When we express sincere gratitude for what we have in our lives, we are actively focusing on the positive aspects and opening ourselves up to receive even more blessings.

One of the main reasons gratitude is so essential to manifestation is because it shifts our energy and vibrations. Everything in the universe operates on vibrations, including our thoughts, emotions, and desires. When we feel grateful, we raise our vibrational frequency to align with the things we desire. This higher frequency allows us to attract and manifest those desires more effortlessly.

Furthermore, gratitude helps us maintain a positive mindset, which is crucial for successful manifestation. When we focus on what we're grateful for, we shift our attention away from lack or scarcity and towards abundance. This positive shift in perspective enables us to see opportunities, possibilities, and solutions that may have been hidden before.

Gratitude also fosters a sense of contentment and fulfillment in our lives. When we genuinely appreciate what we already have, we avoid the trap of constantly chasing external validation or material possessions. This contentment creates a state of abundance consciousness, where we believe that there is always more than enough to go around. This mindset attracts limitless opportunities and resources into our lives.

As you now know, scientific research has shown that gratitude has numerous benefits for our mental and physical well-being, which directly impacts the manifestation process. You have just surveyed a few of the numerous studies that confirm that people who regularly practice gratitude experience reduced stress levels, improved sleep quality, increased happiness, and enhanced overall well-being. When we feel good, we naturally attract more positive experiences and opportunities.

Incorporating gratitude into the manifestation process can be as simple as my *upon waking rule* or keeping a daily gratitude journal, where you write down things you're grateful for each day. This helps to train your mind to focus on the positive aspects of your life. You can also use gratitude affirmations or practices such as gratitude meditation to deepen your connection to gratitude and amplify its manifestation power.

But, the number one reason gratitude is powerful in manifesting, especially when doing a manifestation meditation, is because gratitude is the highest form of receiving.

JOURNAL AND WORKBOOK ACTIVITIES

1. Challenge yourself to engage in gratitude journaling every morning or evening, recording at least three things in your life you are grateful for.

2. Once this becomes a habit, you can easily incorporate my *upon waking* rule, automatically reflecting on gratitude the moment you open your eyes in the morning.

3. Make sure to attach emotion to your thoughts of gratitude, deeply feeling all the positive emotions associated with your thoughts.

Chapter 14

Cracking the Code: The Secrets for Vibrant Health and Healing

"Belief is the strongest medicine." - Ralph Waldo Emerson

The Placebo Effect: You Have the Power Within

Have you heard of the Placebo Effect? It's an intriguing phenomenon that occurs when a medical study is conducted. The placebo effect refers to the beneficial effects experienced by individuals who are administered an inactive treatment, such as a sugar pill or a saline injection, with the belief that it is an actual therapeutic intervention. Typically, one control group in the study receives the medication that is being tested, while the other control group receives a sugar pill, commonly referred to as a placebo. Despite lacking any active ingredients or direct physiological effects, the placebo treatment often elicits positive changes in a patient's symptoms, physiology, and overall well-being.

In these blind studies, participants are not told which control group they are in. Surprisingly, a significant percentage of the people in these studies are healed without taking the actual drug designed to heal them. Why? How can that be? What's going on here? This unique and intriguing response has garnered significant attention and recognition in medical research due to its potential for promoting healing and its implications for understanding the mind-body connection.

The placebo effect shows us that the mind has a profound impact on healing. When people believe they are taking something that will make them better, their bodies respond accordingly, even if the medicine is just a sugar pill. The placebo effect is recognized for its ability to produce clinically significant improvements in patient outcomes, even when compared to active treatments.

In several clinical trials, researchers have observed placebo treatments achieving comparable or sometimes even superior results to active interventions, such as medications or surgical procedures. This observation raises questions about the true efficacy of some medical interventions and emphasizes the need to consider the psychological and neurobiological factors involved in patient healing. Validating the placebo effect in such scenarios implies that harnessing the power of the mind and beliefs can be an effective strategy for promoting recovery.

The magic here lies in the power of belief. It is an accepted phenomenon that medical science has studied, tested, and confirmed. And it is recognized by the medical community and research organizations who must plan for it and adjust their findings accordingly. One of the primary reasons why the placebo effect is recognized as a valid method for healing is its consistent manifestation across various medical conditions and interventions.

Numerous studies have documented the placebo response in diverse fields, ranging from pain management, psychiatric disorders, and neurological conditions, to name a few. These findings highlight the broad applicability of the placebo effect across different healthcare domains, underscoring its importance in understanding the intricacies of healing mechanisms.

Moreover, the placebo effect has been extensively investigated through rigorous scientific methodologies, employing double-blind, placebo-controlled trials, which are widely regarded as the gold standard in medical research. These studies minimize bias and confounding variables by randomly assigning participants to either receive the active treatment or the placebo, without their knowledge. By comparing the outcomes of both groups, researchers can determine the placebo effect's contribution to the observed improvements, making the recognition of its validity even more compelling.

Additionally, advancements in neuroimaging techniques have allowed scientists to delve deeper into understanding the mechanisms underlying the placebo effect. Functional magnetic resonance imaging (fMRI) studies have revealed that placebo treatments can modulate the activity of specific brain regions implicated in pain processing, mood regulation, and immune responses. These neurobiological findings provide concrete evidence of the placebo effect's impact on the neuronal pathways involved in healing, further substantiating its recognition as a valid method for promoting well-being.

It may sound unbelievable, but it is true. You do not need to be part of a blind study to use the power of your thoughts to heal yourself of various ailments. The incredible power of belief is all you need. Are you listening? This is fact, based on science.

Quantum Healing

But it doesn't stop there. Quantum healing takes this concept to a whole new level. If quantum physics tells us that the quantum field is a realm of infinite possibilities, then why couldn't it play a role in the possibility of healing ourselves? This field of energy and potential could hold the key to unlocking our body's natural ability to heal itself beyond the placebo effect. Quantum physics tells us that everything in the universe is made up of energy and that this energy is interconnected. It makes perfect sense that when tapping into this field and harnessing its healing energy, we can heal ourselves from a variety of ailments. Using the power of belief and shifting our thoughts and intentions, we can create a space for healing to occur on a quantum level, affecting our physical bodies in profound ways.

Quantum Healing, also known as Quantum Energy Healing or Quantum Medicine, is a holistic approach to healing that integrates principles from quantum physics and various healing modalities. In simple terms, quantum healing is based on the principle that everything in the universe, including our bodies, is made from an unfathomable amount of subatomic particles that are constantly vibrating and emitting energy. These particles interact and exchange information with each other, creating a complex web of energy patterns within and around us. It is based on the understanding that everything in the universe, including our bodies, is composed of energy fields. Quantum Healing operates on the belief that by manipulating these energy fields, one can stimulate the body's natural healing mechanisms and promote overall well-being.

When these energy patterns become imbalanced or disrupted, it can lead to physical, emotional, and psychological symptoms.

Quantum healing seeks to identify and correct these imbalances by restoring the flow of energy and information in a holistic and non-invasive manner. Practitioners of quantum healing utilize various techniques such as energy healing, meditation, visualization, and intention setting to facilitate the body's natural healing mechanisms. They believe that by consciously directing and influencing the energy within and around the body, a person can stimulate their own innate healing abilities and restore optimal health.

Additionally, quantum healing recognizes the profound influence of consciousness on our well-being. It embraces the notion that our thoughts, beliefs, and emotions directly impact our physical health. By promoting positive and empowering states of mind, such as gratitude, love, and joy, quantum healing aims to create a harmonious environment within the body that supports healing and overall wellness.

One prominent figure who recognizes the merits of Quantum Healing is Dr. Deepak Chopra, a well-respected physician and advocate for integrative medicine. Dr. Chopra has extensively written about the mind-body connection and the role that consciousness plays in healing. He integrates concepts of quantum physics into his work, emphasizing the influence of thoughts, intentions, and beliefs on the body's ability to heal.

Gregg Braden is a well-known figure who explores the intersection of science and spirituality. In his book "The Divine Matrix," Braden delves into the concept of quantum healing. He emphasizes that our thoughts, emotions, and beliefs can influence the energy that surrounds us, potentially leading to healing. Braden often refers to scientific studies, such as those conducted by the Institute of HeartMath, to support his claims. He also explores the role of coherence and heart-brain interactions in healing processes.

Joe Dispenza has extensively studied the power of the mind and its ability to influence healing and well-being. His book "You Are the Placebo" delves into the concept of utilizing the placebo effect intentionally. Dispenza highlights that our thoughts, intentions, and beliefs have a profound impact on our body's ability to heal. He combines scientific research from fields such as neuroscience and quantum physics to explain the mechanisms behind this process. Dispenza's work revolves around training individuals to tap into their inner healing potential.

Theoretical physicist and author of the book "Quantum Doctor", Dr. Amit Goswami recognizes the validity of quantum healing. Dr. Goswami emphasizes the role of consciousness in healing and highlights the importance of integrating both modern science and ancient spiritual wisdom in understanding and promoting health.

Another well-known figure in the scientific community who acknowledges the potential of quantum healing is Dr. Bruce Lipton, a cellular biologist and author of the book "The Biology of Belief". Dr. Lipton explores the impact of thoughts, intentions, and beliefs on our biology, highlighting the pivotal role of our mind in shaping our physical health.

Fritjof Capra, a physicist and systems theorist, has deepened our understanding of the connections between quantum physics, spirituality, and healing. In his seminal book "The Tao of Physics," Capra suggests that the principles of quantum physics, such as non-locality and interconnectedness, align with ancient wisdom traditions and offer a new framework for understanding healing. While Capra's work is not focused solely on quantum healing, he provides valuable insights into the philosophical and theoretical foundations that underpin the concept.

Although more known for his humor and satirical approach, Steve Bhaerman has also contributed to the exploration of quantum healing. Through his alter ego, "Swami Beyondananda", Bhaerman combines spirituality and humor to shed light on the power of intention and consciousness. While his work may not directly involve extensive scientific research, it serves to bring attention to the idea that healing can occur through shifts in perspective and a sense of interconnectedness.

The Institute of Noetic Sciences (IONS), a research organization dedicated to exploring the frontiers of consciousness and healing, has also shown support for Quantum Healing. This organization investigates various unconventional healing practices, including energy medicine and mind-body approaches. Through empirical research and rigorous scientific methodologies, IONS examines the effects of these practices on health outcomes and well-being.

Quantum Healing has also found recognition in the field of quantum biology, which explores the intersection between quantum physics and biology. Research in quantum biology suggests that quantum phenomena, such as coherence and entanglement, may indeed play a role in biological processes, including healing. This emerging field has prompted scientists and researchers to further investigate the potential applications of quantum mechanics in healing.

Furthermore, a growing number of healthcare providers and practitioners are incorporating quantum healing methods into their practice. Integrative medicine, which combines conventional medicine with complementary and alternative therapies, is gaining recognition and acceptance in the medical community. Quantum healing techniques, such as meditation, energy healing, and visualization, are often used as supportive therapies alongside conventional treatment approaches.

It is important to note that while quantum healing can be utilized as a complementary approach to conventional medicine, it is not intended to replace professional medical advice or treatments. It is always recommended to consult with qualified healthcare providers for diagnosis, treatment, and management of any medical condition.

Meditation and Brain Power

Meditation is another powerful tool to consider for self healing. We already know that our thoughts have a direct impact on our physical bodies. Engaging in a meditation where we purposefully direct our thoughts to believe and focus on the idea of healing, should amplify our power, thus enabling the cells of our bodies to respond accordingly and correct any malady that has befallen us. We also are now aware that studies on the brain have revealed the incredible potential of neural plasticity, showing that our brains can indeed help heal themselves. It's empowering to realize that we have the ability to heal ourselves using meditation as a tool to manifest vibrant health.

Now, this is not to say that we should completely abandon western medical practices. There is a time and place for medication and surgeries, especially in emergency situations. If my arm is suddenly cut off, it would be ludicrous to simply sit down and try to meditate it back together. In cases of acute injuries or severe illnesses, immediate medical attention is crucial. However, it is also important to recognize that there are alternative methods of healing that can complement traditional medicine. By combining the best of both worlds, we can optimize our healing potential and live in optimum health.

As for brain power, the brain's ability to influence cellular behavior extends beyond the realms of basic physiology. Research has shown that our thoughts, emotions, and beliefs can have a profound impact on our health and well-being. The field of Psychoneuroimmunology (PNI) explores the intricate connections between the mind, the nervous system, and the immune system, demonstrating how psychological factors can influence immune system function and overall health.

Within the medical community PNI has also explored the link between the mind and the body's healing capabilities. PNI investigates how our thoughts, emotions, and beliefs affect our immune system and overall well-being. PNI provides a scientific foundation for understanding the mind-body connection and the potential influence of our internal states on healing processes. Moreover, the field of psychoneuroimmunology, focuses on the nervous system and immune system, and sheds light on the impact of our thoughts and emotions on our overall well-being.

Additionally, the concept of neuroplasticity highlights the brain's remarkable ability to reorganize and adapt in response to experiences and environmental stimuli. It suggests that our thoughts, habits, and mindset can shape the structure and function of our brains, ultimately influencing our behaviors and outcomes. Our brains are incredibly adaptable and have the ability to form new neural connections throughout our lives. By consistently focusing our thoughts and emotions on healing, we can stimulate the growth of new neural pathways dedicated to promoting health and well-being.

The concept of utilizing the power of the brain to influence physiological processes within the body is not as far-fetched as it may initially seem. Over the years, extensive research has been conducted in the field of mind-body medicine, exploring the potential of mental and emotional states in promoting healing and well-being. The brain plays a significant role in modulating various bodily functions, including the immune response, inflammation, and even pain perception. By harnessing the power of the mind and utilizing techniques such as visualization and meditation, individuals can potentially enhance their body's natural healing mechanisms and promote an environment conducive to recovery.

The brain, as the control center of the human body, communicates with different areas through a complex network of nerves. This communication occurs via neurotransmitters and electrical impulses, resulting in a myriad of physiological responses. Our mental and emotional states have the ability to impact this intricate communication network, potentially influencing the functioning of organs, cells, and even genes.

The brain's influence can be harnessed to support the healing process. The field of psychoneuroimmunology (PNI) has extensively investigated the interaction between psychological factors, the nervous system, and the immune system. Research within the field has demonstrated that psychological stressors can negatively affect immune function, leaving individuals more susceptible to developing diseases or experiencing prolonged healing times. Conversely, positive emotions, relaxation techniques, and a generally positive mindset have been correlated with enhanced immune function and improved overall health outcomes.

To effectively leverage the mind's potential for healing, utilizing various mind-body techniques can be beneficial. Meditation, for instance, cultivates a state of deep relaxation and mental focus. During meditation another effective technique to add in is visualization. While meditating, visualization involves creating detailed mental images of the desired outcome, allowing the brain to perceive them as real experiences. By visualizing the healing of a particular area in your body, you can direct your brain to engage in processes that support that intent.

When we truly believe in our ability to heal, our mind triggers a cascade of biochemical and neurological processes that work in harmony to initiate a powerful healing response. This is not mere wishful thinking; it is the profound convergence of intention, emotion, and physiological changes within our bodies.

One of the key principles here is the power of intention and conscious thought in influencing the cells of our bodies. Our thoughts are not merely intangible ideas floating in our minds; they have the ability to shape our reality, including our physical well-being. Our thoughts and emotions create electromagnetic fields around us, which have a direct impact on our physiology. When we consciously direct our thoughts towards healing and vibrant health, we are essentially instructing our brains to communicate with the cells of our body in a transformative way. Through dedicated practice, we can train our brains to generate healing.

It is also important to become aware of our unconscious thoughts and beliefs, as they can sabotage our efforts to manifest better health. By identifying and rewiring these deeply ingrained patterns of thinking, we can remove the barriers that hinder our healing journey.

Facing the Facts, My Personal Testament

I personally experienced the power of healing through meditation when I went through one of the most stressful years of my life. I was commuting long distances to a highly stressful job, and as a result of this stress, I developed adult acne breakouts that seemed impossible to get rid of. It was during this time that I discovered the secrets of healing through meditation.

I remember the first time I did this. I had horribly painful underground acne cysts on my forehead and my nose was congested with puss filled bacteria, resulting in hideous blemishes. My extreme breakouts would not respond to the numerous acne facial cleansers, antiseptics, and topical medications I wasted my money on. It was about five days before my finance (at the time) and I were flying out to Michigan with my oldest son to go see my youngest son who had a leading role in a play at his university.

It was an important trip for me as our little family had not spent quality time together for a long while, because my oldest had moved into his first apartment and my youngest was still away at his university. I wanted the weekend to be special and I didn't want my sons to see their mom in such a state or be embarrassed by my appearance. We would be meeting with the other parents we had come to know and I was introducing my fiance to them. I just had to do something to clear up my skin.

I took the time to make a recording of a guided meditation script I was able to obtain. It was one of Dr. Joe Dispenza's, which I knew to be a very powerful tool he had used on patients who partnered with him to be a part of his research studies on self healing. I did this lengthy meditation, almost an hour long, for four consecutive days. On each of these mornings, I had to get up at "dark thirty" in order to have time to make the morning commute to work. Miraculously, it was like my skin transformed before my eyes and by the time we got on the airplane, my skin was clear and radiant and remained so for the entire glorious weekend!

However, when I returned to work, so did the acne. I now know that this was because I was under unrelenting pressure and ignoring my stress. As a result, the harmful hormones and chemicals produced by my chronic stress manifested in the return of my acne breakouts. And while I wish I would have had my wits about me back then, deep down I knew I was able to manifest clear skin whenever I needed to look my best. And that's exactly what I did.

Despite the fact that my skin continued to rebel against me and I chose to just live with it, I performed my powerful meditation right prior to some pretty big events that were scheduled during this hectic year. I attended two societal balls with my husband, several weekend cruises with the yacht club, and was the emcee to an audience of parents and teachers at my school at the performance of a children's singing and dance recital I choreographed and directed every year.

In between these big events, I was powerless to control my stress levels due to exhaustion. I simply didn't have the time. I woke up at 4:30 AM every morning and drove 70 miles to my high stress job teaching 5th grade. If you aren't aware of how it is for teachers let me expand. First, there is no real "downtime" as a teacher. I was continually "on" with about 30 or so ten-year-olds, all needing my attention, not to mention the unusual amount of behavior problems in my class that year.

The aftermath of distance learning during the Covid pandemic, greatly impacted the social norms of children who basically had zero social and emotional experience of how to be in a classroom setting. This made classroom management extremely difficult, as teachers nationwide had to teach this specific behavior that is normally addressed in the primary grades.

On top of this I had an alarming amount of children in my classroom who suffered from extreme emotional trauma. Some exhibited outlandish and odd habitual behaviors. And a good many resorted to emotionally charged outbreaks or tantrums, if you will, that were bewildering and upsetting, not only to me, but to the other kids witnessing it and to many other staff or intervention teachers assigned to mentor these kids. I can honestly say, I've never seen anything like it before in my 26 years of teaching.

Of course, I finally realized that addressing the underlying stressors in my life was essential for long-term healing. Ultimately, I made the decision to resign from teaching at the end of the school year, eliminate the absurd commute, and find a healthier environment to work in.

However, this ordeal was actually a blessing in disguise. If I hadn't experienced it, I might not have learned many of the things I am presenting in this book. I might not have read and researched many of these topics, particularly the information in this chapter.

Yes, I learned how to manifest clear skin anytime I wished, almost like magic. I learned firsthand the power I had within me to manifest and heal myself. And I'm not alone. Many people have experienced similar results through the power of this healing practice. Although it may not be a solution for every ailment, integrating these methods into our lives can bring about incredible transformations.

According to Chopra

According to Deepak Chopra, the root cause of disease can often be traced back to imbalance or disharmony in these different aspects of our being. He likes to make people aware of the actual word disease, stressing how it defines itself as *dis-"ease"*. The "ease" with which we should be aligned, becomes imbalanced and thus the negative influences can sabotage our health with *disease*.

Chopra asserts that our consciousness, which encompasses our thoughts, beliefs, and intentions, plays a crucial role in shaping our physical reality. By cultivating a positive and optimistic mindset, we can activate our body's natural healing mechanisms and facilitate the restoration of balance. Embracing meditation, visualization, and harnessing the power of our mind-body connection, we can unlock an extraordinary potential for healing.

Furthermore, Chopra encourages individuals to embrace a holistic lifestyle that incorporates healthy habits and practices. This includes maintaining a nutritious diet, engaging in regular physical activity, getting adequate sleep, and managing stress effectively. According to him, these lifestyle choices promote optimal well-being and strengthen the body's innate healing abilities and immune systems.

In addition to these principles, Chopra often incorporates various ancient practices into his teachings, such as Ayurveda, meditation, and Yoga. Ayurveda, a traditional Indian system of medicine, focuses on restoring balance in the body through personalized dietary and lifestyle recommendations. Meditation and yoga, on the other hand, help to calm the mind, reduce stress, and improve overall health.

It is important to note that while Deepak Chopra's teachings emphasize the power of the mind-body connection in healing, he always advocates for an integrated approach to healthcare. He believes in the importance of working with qualified healthcare professionals and utilizing conventional medical treatments when necessary.

You are in Control

So, who is in control of your health and healing? The simple answer is you. You have the power to take charge of your own well-being and explore different methods of healing. The power to heal yourself lies within you. By harnessing the power of your thoughts, beliefs, and intentions, you can tap into your body's natural healing abilities. While modern western medical practices have their place, exploring alternative methods of healing can enhance our overall health and well-being. The placebo effect, the principles of quantum physics, the power of belief, your brain and neuroplasticity, and the practice of meditation, all support the idea that we can influence our physical well-being.

Remember, you too have the power to heal yourself through the incredible potential of your brain. Using visualization in your meditations for healing, from mild skin problems to other diseases, we can live in the abundance of vibrant health.

JOURNAL AND WORKBOOK ACTIVITIES

Try it out for yourself. Start with something simple, maybe a headache or any kind of mild pain. The skin or your fingernails can be a fairly easy part of our bodies to alter. Maybe you have some sort of rash, a mild burn, acne, a hang nail, or short thin nails you will wish were longer and stronger.

Do this meditation every day until the healing is manifested. You may decide to make a guided recording to use at first.

Meditation to Manifest Healing - Outline

1. Quiet your mind and focus on breathing. Take several deep breaths in through the nose, hold the breath at the top, then release the breath slowly out the nose. Whisper silently in your mind the words breathe in and breathe out or count with numbers in order to control your mind from wandering.

2. Focus on pure consciousness. Tell yourself: "I am in the present moment. This is the now." Repeat this mantra until you are feeling connected to pure consciousness.

3. Visualize your body floating upward, passing through the ceiling and the roof of your home. Continue upward slowly, looking down at your neighborhood. As you rise further upward continue to peer down on the landscape as if you are in an airplane. Pass through the clouds and continue slowly upward until you are in deep dark space. In the vast darkness of space, let the stars and galaxies disappear. You are now floating in the quantum field.

4. Tell yourself: "I release my ego and perceptions of who I think I am. In this moment, I am no one, with no body, no where, in

no time". Repeat and visualize until you feel detached from this world.

5. Visualize the constructs of all the energy in you and around you. This can look however you want it to. Visualize becoming one with the energy, vibrating with it, and feel its power.

6. In your mind say and BELIEVE: "I surrender to the void of the unknown. I am in the realm of limitless potential. I am connected to the source of all possibilities." Repeat this until you feel connected to the quantum field.

7. Now it is time to focus your attention on what you want to heal. Visualize this part of the body and slowly zoom in on it, until you are so close that you can see the cells and subatomic particles it is composed of.

8. Then fill it up with a vibrating swirl of any color you want. This energy is the healing energy that will transform and heal you. Feel its warmth and power. Continue this visualization for several minutes.

9. Tell your brain: "I need you to send out signals to my cells and have my cells descend upon (part of body you are healing). I need you to instruct the cells to remedy (part of body you are healing) and completely eliminate what ails me. I need you to tell my cells not to stop working until I am completely healed. Thank you for doing this, as this is your job." Repeat until you are convinced the cells have begun the healing.

10. Thank the Divine Intelligence for granting your wish. Visualize yourself already healed. You are in some future moment. Be specific as you imagine where you are, who you are with, and what you are doing or saying. Make it detailed and real.

11. Deeply begin to feel your emotions in this imagined moment. Focus on the joy, relief, happiness, fulfillment, and all the

positive emotions that come up for you. Feel these emotions so intensely that you will never forget this moment, in this meditation, where you have received your desire from the universe that truly wants to give this to you.

12. End your session focusing on gratitude. Let the quantum field know that you are grateful to be able to access its field of energy and possibilities. Thank the universe for granting your desire. Focus on all the things in your life that you already have and how grateful you are that they came to you out of the unity of consciousness that loves you and is love itself.

13. When you are ready, end your meditation and open your eyes. Go through your days practicing gratitude, as it is the highest form of receiving. Know that what you asked for has already been given to you. Do not let thoughts of doubt cross your mind.

Chapter 15

Illuminating the Energy Centers: Discovering Your Chakras

"The chakras are like the wheels of a clock, each one contributing to the symphony of our being." - Donna Eden

Wheels of Fortune

The word "chakra" is derived from the Sanskrit word for wheel. In Hinduism and other belief systems, these wheels are centers of energy that reside in different parts of the body. These energy centers were first mentioned in ancient spiritual texts known as the Vedas dating back as far as 1500 to 100 BC.

There are seven main chakras located along an energetic channel from the base of the spine to the crown of the head. Each chakra has a different function and color, each one associated with a specific element and physical organ in the body.

Energy or *prana* in the yogic tradition flows through the chakras. These chakras act as junction points between our human form and consciousness. When chakras are balanced, energy flows freely, energizing and revitalizing the body.

There are unique and specific ways to balance each chakra, including practices for increasing the energy of a chakra when it is too low, and practices for calming the energy of a chakra when it is too high. By working with the chakras, you can improve your physical health, emotional well-being, and spiritual growth.

When our chakras are out of balance, it can lead to stress, anxiety, and depression. Balancing chakras is the process of tending to these areas of our body through the power of our thoughts so that we may feel more aligned and healthy. If your chakras are out of balance, you may experience difficulties with mood, focus, and overall health.

The first three chakras are associated with your physical experience in the local world, while the last four chakras are associated with your spiritual experience in the non-local world.

It is suggested by many practitioners to focus on the bottom three chakras first before moving on to the others. Regardless, all the chakras have a healing intention, and by understanding and working with these intentions, we can bring our chakras back into harmony, allowing energy to flow freely and manifest vibrant health.

The Chakra system offers a holistic approach to understanding ourselves and our place in the world. Each chakra is associated with specific qualities and aspects of our existence, acting as a roadmap to balance and enhance the flow of energy in our lives.

The Secrets of the Chakras

First Chakra	Root Chakra	*Muladhara*

Situated at the base of our spine

Element - earth

Color - Red

Mantra - *Lam*

This Chakra grounds us, connecting us to the earth's nurturing energy. It governs our survival instincts, stability, and sense of belonging and grounding. It is connected to courage and self-care.

Second Chakra	Sacral Chakra	*Svadhisthana*

Situated at the area of the pelvis

Element - Water

Color - Orange

Mantra - *Vam*

Moving up, we encounter the Sacral Chakra, nestled in the lower abdomen. This vibrant energy center governs our passions and sexual energy. It is the driving force behind our desires and emotional well-being. Creativity and pleasure stem from this energy center.

Third Chakra	Solar Plexus Chakra	*Manipura*

Situated just above the navel

Element - Fire

Color - Yellow

Mantra - *Ram*

Next on our journey is the Solar Plexus Chakra, located in the upper abdomen. This powerhouse Chakra governs our personal power, confidence, and self-esteem. It ignites the fire of our willpower and propels us toward our goals. It is associated with transformation.

Fourth Chakra	Heart Chakra	*Ahahata*

Situated in the chest area

Element - Air

Color - Green

Mantra - *Yam*

Ascending further, we arrive at the Heart Chakra, situated in the center of our chest. This radiant Chakra is the beacon of love, compassion, forgiveness, peace and harmony. It nurtures our relationships from romantic love to self-love and empathy for all beings.

Fifth Chakra	Throat Chakra	*Vishuddha*

Situated at the throat

Element - *akasha* (Sanskrit for space or pure potentiality)

Color - Blue

Mantra - *Ham*

Continuing our ascent, we reach the Throat Chakra, conveniently placed at our throat. This communication hub governs our ability to express ourselves, both verbally and non-verbally. It is our authentic voice, whether speaking, writing, or communicating through the arts. It grants us the power to speak our truth and listen deeply.

Sixth Chakra	Third Eye Chakra	*Ajna*

Situated at the center of your forehead

Element - earth

Color - Purple

Mantra - *Sham*

Climbing higher still, we arrive at the enchanting Third Eye Chakra, nestled between our eyebrows. This mystical eye enhances our intuition, insight, perception, and inner vision. It is connected to decisions and choice making. It guides us to see beyond the surface, tapping into the infinite wisdom of the universe. There is nothing the Third Eye can not see.

Seventh Chakra	Crown Chakra	*Sahaswara*

Situated at the crown of your head or floating just above your head

Element - Spirit or Source or Collective Consciousness

Color - White or Ultra-Violet

Mantra - *Om*

Finally, we stand in awe before the Crown Chakra, majestically seated at the top of our head and maybe floating a little above. This ethereal gateway connects us to the divine, cosmic energy of the quantum field. It grants us access to higher states of unity consciousness, enlightenment, spiritual awakening and transcendence.

JOURNAL AND WORKBOOK ACTIVITIES

Buy or make a chart of the chakras. You could also look it up online and print one out. Make sure it is in color or take the time to color it. Keep it where you meditate for reference.

Try to become familiar with each chakra name, color, location on your body and basic attributes.

Chapter 16

Balanced Abundance: Aligning Your Chakras Boosts Manifestation

"In every culture and in every medical tradition before ours, healing was accomplished by moving energy." - Albert Szent-Györgyi

Guided meditations for chakra alignment are an extraordinary tool for anyone seeking to activate and balance their chakras in a profound and transformative way.

Every thought and emotion we experience produces an electrical and magnetic signature, which in turn creates a corresponding electromagnetic field around us. These electromagnetic fields have a direct influence on our lives and attract similar frequencies from the quantum field.

By visualizing ourselves as *no one*, with *no body*, and in no specific location or *no where*, we dismantle the habitual patterns of thought and emotion that have created our current reality. We break free from the old stories about ourselves that hold us back from living our best lives. This state of detachment allows us to create a void, an empty space, where new and more empowering thoughts and emotions can emerge.

It also helps us detach from the outcomes or desires we are manifesting. When we are too attached to a specific outcome, we create resistance and limit the flow of abundance and manifestation. By surrendering our desires to the quantum field and detaching from any expectations, we open ourselves to receiving something even greater than we could have imagined.

Utilizing guided meditation for chakra alignment is a powerful tool that can help you achieve a state of balance. By following this carefully designed meditation practice, you will be able to manifest more effectively.

Meditation in this intentional and immersive manner lets you bypass any limiting beliefs or energetic blockages that may be hindering the alignment of your chakras. It helps you tap into your innate potential and access higher states of consciousness, where holistic healing and personal growth can thrive.

Through this practice, myself, and countless individuals have experienced profound transformation, joy, and fulfillment. So, I encourage you to give it a try and see the incredible results for yourself.

You might want to record your voice and use it as a guide to walk yourself through this guided meditation. Pause between each paragraph to allow silent time during your meditation.

Guided Chakra Visualization Script

1. "Close your eyes and embrace the silence as you enter a world of focused relaxation. In this state, your mind becomes

a gateway to the subconscious, where your chakras reside. By accessing this realm of heightened awareness, you open the door to unlimited possibilities and begin the process of aligning your chakras."

2. "Imagine a powerful mental movie unfolding before your eyes. Picture yourself starting at the base of the spine, where the root chakra resides. Visualize its vibrant red color and see it as a spinning ball of energy. Feel its energy vibrating inside you, filling every fiber of your being and finally radiating outward to the space around you. The root chakra grounds you and gives you stability in your life. Meditate here until you feel aligned."

3. "Now, move up to the sacral chakra, situated in the pelvis area, where your lower belly is. Envisioning its captivating orange hue. As you see this ball of energy spinning, feel a warm and comforting sensation spreading through your body. The sacral chakra holds your passion, your creativity, and your sexual energy. Meditate here until you feel aligned."

4. "Next in line is the Sacral chakra, located just above your navel in the upper abdomen. Picture a bright yellow ball, almost like a miniature sun spinning and vibrating inside you. This chakra governs your personal power, confidence, and self esteem. It is associated with transformation. Feel and honor the power of the sacral chakra. Meditate here until you feel aligned."

5. "Now elevate your attention to your Heart chakra and fill the area around your heart with a vibrant green sphere. This spectacular chakra is the beacon of love, compassion, and empathy. Let every feeling of love in your life radiate here and remove any ill feelings toward anyone, allowing the power of the Heart chakra to consume you as you practice forgiveness and welcome in peace and harmony. Meditate here until you feel aligned."

6. "Continuing your ascent, rest your focus on the area around your throat, and envision the spinning blue ball here that is your Throat chakra. Here you can find your authentic voice and ability to express yourself both verbally and nonverbally. This chakra governs your communication and makes it more effective. Meditate here until you feel aligned."

7. "Climbing higher still, you arrive at the enchanting Third Eye Chakra, nestled between your eyebrows. Visualize a brilliant, glowing purple ball in the middle of your forehead. The mystical eye enhances your intuition, your insight, and your inner vision. Let this ball expand to fill your whole head. The Third Eye chakra can tap into the infinite wisdom of the universe and is correlated with supernatural powers. There is nothing your Third Eye can not see. Meditate here until you feel aligned."

8. "Finally, envision a floating orb on the top of your head or better yet, floating just above your head. This spinning orb is a luminous, almost iridescent, white or ultraviolet. This is your majestic Crown chakra, the ethereal gateway connecting you to the divine, cosmic energy of the quantum field. Meditate here until you feel aligned."

9. "Now picture all your chakras in a perfect line, growing bigger and bigger. Allow each ball of energy to expand outward from your body, radiating energy to the space around you. Visualize each chakra being in perfect alignment, with the vibrations of each spinning ball of energy felt deeply within you."

10. "Now you have stimulated and activated each of the seven chakras. Visualize yourself floating up into the atmosphere, higher and higher until you find yourself in the depths of deep, dark space. In this ethereal realm, visualize becoming no one, with no body and in no place. Release your sense of identity, your limitations, and your attachments to the physical world.

Let go of your ego and all preconceived notions of who you are, creating space for new possibilities to emerge."

11. "In this state of detachment, you tap into the vast potential of the quantum field. Everything is interconnected, and all possibilities exist simultaneously. By releasing your physical existence, you unlock the ability to connect with these infinite potentials beyond your limited perception."

Now that your Chakras are energized and aligned you can end the meditation, or you can continue the meditation and manifest something you desire or ask for healing.

JOURNAL AND WORKBOOK ACTIVITIES

- Make an audio recording of your voice, as a guided meditation, following the "Guided Chakra Visualization Script" previously outlined. By using your own guided meditation, over time, you will be able to walk yourself through the steps without needing the script.
- Examine your chakras as outlined below.
- Follow any suggestions to realign.
- It's important to note that experiencing these signs does not necessarily mean that a specific chakra is blocked or imbalanced. However, if you're consistently experiencing multiple symptoms related to a particular chakra, it may be worth exploring ways to balance and heal it along with Guided Chakra Meditation.

CHAKRA BALANCE CHECKLIST

ROOT CHAKRA in Balance: Allows you to feel grounded and confident.

Excess Energy: Leads to greed and cockiness.

The Fix: Practice forgiveness, get rid of items you no longer need, get a pedicure

Low Energy: Feeling unhinged or disconnected from your job, family, true self.

The Fix: Read, walk barefoot in nature, dance, exercise, garden

SACRAL CHAKRA in Balance: Allows you to feel comfortable in your own skin and accepting of your emotions. It also allows for creative expression of self.

Excess Energy: You may look past your faults and become hyper focused on pleasure. It can lead to excessive indulging and co-dependence.

The Fix: put clear boundaries around relationships at home and work, try acupressure or Reiki

Low Energy: Can lead to creative blocks, feeling unloved, and emotional roller coasters.

The Fix: Spend time near water, massage, journaling, do something that feels like play

SOLAR PLEXUS CHAKRA in Balance: High self-esteem, strong charisma, and confident decision making

Excess Energy: Tempers may flare and you may feel a need to control everything and everyone.

The Fix: Drink only room-temperature beverages, take slow calming breaths, try a session in a floatation tank

Low Energy: Poor appetite, anxiety, disorganization, and difficulty staying on task.

The Fix: Enjoy spicy foods, get out in the sunshine, wear gold

HEART CHAKRA in Balance: You experience compassion, love, and acceptance.

Excess Energy: Experiencing jealousy or feeling clingy.

The Fix: Write a letter of gratitude, put your attention on uplifting emotions such as compassion, joy, and tenderness, look through an old photo album and savor your memories

Low Energy: Feeling shy or lonely, or experiencing an inability to forgive.

The Fix: Watch a romantic movie, use the affirmation "I deeply and completely love myself", wear pink quartz, dab rose essential oil on your wrists, try a loving kindness meditation

THROAT CHAKRA in Balance: You feel authentic and are a confident conversationalist and good listener.

Excess Energy: An emotional overload, all choked up, also associated with manipulative behavior, arrogance, and being too talkative.

The Fix: Listen, drink warm tea, journal or write (rather than speak)

Low Energy: Tendency to feel shy or reticent or to act in a passive-aggressive way.

The Fix: Sing, chant, speak your opinions even when they might be unpopular

THIRD EYE CHAKRA in Balance: Imagination, clairvoyance, synchronicity, and intuition.

Excess Energy: The mind races, you feel that buzzy energy of over-caffeination or sleeplessness, it can be difficult to concentrate or stay on task.

The Fix: Enjoy the scent of sage or sandalwood, spend time under the moon and stars

Low Energy: Impedes your ability to remember and concentrate, processing speed slows and you may be prone to indecision and procrastination.

The Fix: Spend time in the sun, explore and release limiting beliefs, pay attention to your dreams

CROWN CHAKRA in Balance: Self-awareness, wisdom, and connection to the inner compass that guides you to your highest self.

Excess Energy: Materialism and rigid self-identity

The Fix: Witness your thoughts rather than getting caught up in them, wear white

Low Energy: leads to depression, a sense of disconnection from life, and a lack of compassion.

The Fix: Learn something new, meditate, wear purple

Section Three

ELEVATE

Inspiring Unity

In this section you will learn the basics needed to understand the unity of all things and how this understanding will help you to inspire others. This knowledge is the culmination of all the ideas presented in this book. After gleaning the profound ideas in each chapter, you will become inspired to take what you have learned to a new level. It is imperative to elevate yourself and others with the knowledge and the science you will have acquired from reading this book. This section is designed to expand your horizons, help you find your life's purpose, and open your heart to sharing your gifts with others for the good of all and the harm of none.

Chapter 17

Unity Consciousness: The Ultimate Path

"We are not separate from the universe; we are a part of it. The universe is expressing itself through us." - Carl Sagan

Carl Sagan's belief that we are not separate from the universe but rather a part of it, and that the universe is expressing itself through us, is not just a philosophical idea; it is supported by scientific principles.

The theory of evolution provides further evidence for our connection to the universe. The process of natural selection has shaped life on earth, and through evolution, all living organisms share a common ancestry. This unifying relationship among different species highlights our interconnectedness and the fact that we are a product of the same evolutionary journey as everything else on this planet.

The principles of conservation of energy and matter also support our unity with the universe. According to these principles, energy and matter cannot be created nor destroyed, but merely transformed from one form to another. This implies that the atoms and molecules that make up our bodies were once a part of stars, brought forth through immense cosmic processes. We are literally made of stardust, intimately tied to the vastness of the cosmos.

The study of stellar evolution and nucleosynthesis reveals that the elements that make up our bodies, such as carbon, oxygen, and iron, were formed within the cores of stars through nuclear reactions. This process of stellar nucleosynthesis connects us to the cosmic origins of matter and reinforces our unity with the universe.

Truly, we are not separate observers of the universe, but integral parts of its vast expression.

Unity Consciousness

Unity consciousness is a profound state of awareness where an individual recognizes and experiences the interconnectedness and oneness of all beings and aspects of existence. It is a state of consciousness that transcends egoic boundaries and separateness, allowing us to tap into the deep wisdom and love present in the fabric of the universe. When we live in unity consciousness, we understand that we are not just isolated individuals but rather integral parts of a larger whole.

Living in unity consciousness has the power to enhance your life experiences in countless ways. First and foremost, it brings a sense of deep peace, contentment, and fulfillment. By recognizing that we are all connected and part of something greater, we let go of the need for comparison, competition, and judgment. This leads to a freedom from the constant striving and dissatisfaction that often plague our lives.

Unity consciousness also opens the doors to profound compassion and empathy. When we see others as extensions of ourselves, we naturally feel a deep sense of care and concern for their well-being. We recognize that hurting others ultimately hurts ourselves, and therefore, we are inspired to act with kindness, understanding, and love. This not only enriches our own lives, but it also creates a ripple effect, positively impacting all those around us.

Furthermore, living in unity consciousness allows us to tap into our own innate wisdom and intuition. By transcending the limitations of our ego, we become more attuned to the deeper truths and insights that arise from the collective consciousness. This heightened sense of intuition guides us in making better decisions, finding our life's purpose, and navigating challenges with greater ease and clarity.

Moreover, unity consciousness has the potential to enhance our relationships. When we see others as interconnected parts of ourselves, we cultivate a sense of deep connection and under-standing. This leads to more authentic and fulfilling connections with others, as well as a greater ability to resolve conflicts and create harmonious relationships. Unity consciousness enables us to see beyond the surface level differences and truly connect with the essence of others.

In addition, living in unity consciousness opens us up to a greater sense of abundance and gratitude. When we recognize that we are all part of a vast interconnected web, we realize that the universe is infinitely supportive and abundant. We shift our focus from scarcity and lack to abundance and gratitude, which in turn attracts more positive experiences and opportunities into our lives.

Your Crown Chakra - The Gateway

The Crown Chakra, located at the top of the head, is a gateway to the divine intelligence that exists beyond our physical existence. First and foremost, the Crown Chakra allows us to tap into a higher state of awareness and wisdom. By activating this chakra, we can access a profound level of understanding and knowledge that goes beyond our limited human experience. This expanded consciousness allows us to see things from a broader perspective and make decisions that are aligned with the greater good.

The activation of the Crown Chakra allows us to access higher states of consciousness, such as divine love, bliss, and spiritual ecstasy. These profound experiences go beyond the limitations of our ordinary human existence, offering us glimpses of the infinite and eternal nature of our souls. By entering these elevated states of consciousness, we can tap into the immense power and potential that lies within us, opening doors to creativity, intuition, and inner guidance.

The Crown Chakra is essential for developing our spiritual connection and deepening our relationship with the divine. By expanding our consciousness through this chakra, we establish a direct link with divine intelligence, gaining access to profound insights, guidance, and inspiration. This connection allows us to live in alignment with our soul's purpose and receive divine support in manifesting our desires and fulfilling our potential.

Bliss Consciousness

"Yoga is not about touching your toes, it is what you learn on the way down." - Jigar Gor

Bliss Consciousness in Yoga Philosophy, as explained by Deepak Chopra, is a profound state of being that transcends the limitations of our ordinary human experience. It refers to a state of pure joy, happiness, and contentment that arises when we are connected to our true selves and the higher universal consciousness.

According to Deepak Chopra, Bliss Consciousness is our natural and innate state of being. It is the recognition that our true essence is pure love, joy, and peace. This state is not dependent on external circumstances or achievements; rather, it comes from within, from a deep connection to our innermost self and the divine.

In the *Yoga Sutras* of Patanjali, an ancient text written thousands of years ago, the ultimate goal of yoga is defined as *Samadhi*, which is the state of pure consciousness and bliss.

Bliss Consciousness is attainable through different stages of yoga practice, starting with the physical postures or *asanas*, followed by breath control or *pranayama*, withdrawal of the senses or *pratyahara*, concentration or *dharana*, meditation or *dhyana*, and eventually leading to the state of *Samadhi*.

By regularly practicing these different aspects of yoga, we can quiet the mind, transcend the limitations of our ego, and connect with the divinity that resides within us. It is in this state of expanded awareness that we can experience the pure bliss and limitless possibilities of our consciousness.

JOURNAL AND WORKBOOK ACTIVITIES

Below is a checklist for embracing and nurturing unity consciousness.

- Read through each numbered item and take inventory of each idea reflecting on whether or not it is present in your life.

- Choose one concept a week that you want to focus on.

- In your journal, track your progress and record any significant insights or actions you took to cultivate the concept you focused on each week.

1. Awareness: Start by cultivating an awareness of the interconnectedness and oneness of all beings and aspects of existence. Recognize that we are not separate individuals, but integral parts of a larger whole.

2. Letting go: Release the need for comparison, competition, and judgment. Let go of egoic boundaries and separateness that hinder unity consciousness. Embrace acceptance and non-attachment.

3. Compassion and empathy: Foster a deep sense of care and concern for the well-being of others. Recognize that hurting others ultimately hurts ourselves. Act with kindness, understanding, and love in all interactions.

4. Wisdom and intuition: Transcend the limitations of the ego and tap into your own innate wisdom and intuition. Listen to the deeper truths and insights that arise from the collective consciousness.

5. Authentic connections: Cultivate a sense of deep connection and understanding with others. See beyond surface-level

differences and connect with the essence of others. Strive for authentic and fulfilling relationships.

6. Abundance and gratitude: Shift focus from scarcity and lack to abundance and gratitude. Recognize the infinite support and abundance present in the universe. Practice gratitude daily and attract positive experiences and opportunities into your life.

7. Reflect and self-examine: Continuously reflect on your thoughts, actions, and intentions to align them with unity consciousness. Examine any egoic tendencies or barriers to embracing unity consciousness.

8. Practice mindfulness: Engage in mindfulness practices to stay present and aware of the interconnectedness of all beings. Use mindfulness techniques such as meditation, breathwork, or journaling.

9. Seek inspiration and guidance: Surround yourself with like-minded individuals, read books, listen to podcasts, or attend workshops that inspire and support unity consciousness. Seek guidance from spiritual teachers or mentors.

10. Practice self-love and self-care: Nurture your own well-being and personal growth. Prioritize self-love, self-care, and self-reflection to maintain unity consciousness within yourself.

Chapter 18

The Missing Link: Connecting the Quantum Field and The Divine

"Science without religion is lame, religion without science is blind." - Albert Einstein

Carl Sagan and Albert Einstein, two brilliant minds of the scientific world, have both shared their views on the relationship between religion and science. Their perspectives shed valuable light on the unity that exists between these seemingly different spheres of human understanding.

Sagan, a renowned astronomer and science communicator, believed that science and religion can coexist harmoniously. He recognized the vital role of both in our lives, asserting that science provides us with a methodology to understand the natural world, while religion offers a framework for exploring profound questions of meaning and purpose. Sagan affirmed that these two domains answer distinct aspects of human curiosity and are therefore not inherently incompatible.

One of the most striking aspects of Sagan's views is his

emphasis on the vastness and wonder of the universe. Sagan's popular series "Cosmos" and his book by the same name served to ignite a sense of awe and curiosity in countless individuals. He viewed the exploration of the cosmos not as a threat to religious belief, but as an avenue for spiritual and intellectual growth. For Sagan, the wonders of the universe were a testimony to its intrinsic beauty and harmony, even invoking a sense of reverence that can be seen as deeply spiritual.

Turning our attention to Albert Einstein, the iconic physicist whose theories revolutionized our understanding of the universe, we find a slightly different perspective but one that echoes Sagan's underlying theme of unity. While Einstein did not adhere to any specific religious doctrine, he expressed deep reverence for the natural world and its order. He viewed science as a way to uncover the profound beauty and elegance inherent in the laws of nature.

Einstein's famous quote, "Science without religion is lame, religion without science is blind," captures his belief in their intricate relationship. He argued that a robust religious framework can inspire scientific exploration by posing questions that push us to uncover the underlying mysteries of the universe. Similarly, scientific discoveries, in turn, deepen our awe and appreciation for the profound design and interconnectedness of the cosmos.

In essence, both Sagan and Einstein present a perspective that emphasizes the unity between religion and science. They view religion as a source of meaning and purpose, capable of exploring questions that science alone cannot answer. Simultaneously, they recognize the role of science as a means of unraveling the mysteries of the natural world, fostering a deeper sense of awe and understanding.

The Quantum Connection

The connection between the quantum field and Divine Intelligence, or what many refer to as God, is a captivating concept that has gained significant attention among scientists, philosophers, and spiritual enthusiasts in recent years. The exploration of this connection has unveiled a plethora of fascinating insights that bridge the gap between religion and science, ultimately reshaping our understanding of the universe and our place within it.

Interestingly, numerous parallels can be drawn between the characteristics attributed to Divine Intelligence and the behavior of the quantum field. For instance, both exhibit traits of non-locality and interconnectedness.

Divine Intelligence, commonly associated with God, is the idea that there is a higher, all-encompassing intelligence inherent in the universe. It is the force that orchestrates the unfolding of life, the order behind the chaos, and the wisdom that governs natural laws. Many religious and spiritual traditions speak of this divine presence as a guiding, all-knowing entity that pervades every aspect of existence.

One of the key tenets of quantum physics is the existence of the quantum field, a vast and ever-present field of energy that permeates all of space and time. This field is the underlying fabric of our reality, consisting of infinitesimal particles and waves, constantly interacting and exchanging information. It is within this intricate tapestry of cosmic energy that the connection to Divine Intelligence emerges.

Both the quantum field and Divine Intelligence defy the limitations of time and space and are thus non-local. The quantum field, through principles like superposition and tunneling, allows particles to exist in multiple states simultaneously and traverse through barriers without physical contact. In a similar vein, Divine Intelligence is believed to transcend the confines of time and space, operating beyond our human comprehension of reality.

Entanglement, a fundamental principle of quantum physics, suggests that particles become linked in such a way that their states become intertwined, resulting in an instantaneous influence on one another regardless of the physical distance. This harmony between particles echoes the interconnectedness often associated with Divine Intelligence, where all aspects of creation are intricately linked and influenced by this higher cosmic force.

Philosophical discourse emerging by thought leaders in this arena purpose thought-provoking connections between the quantum field and Divine Intelligence. These parallels and shared characteristics between these concepts present a compelling argument for the existence of a greater universal intelligence aligned with the quantum field.

Religion and Science

Humans throughout history have turned toward religion and spiritual practices to make sense of their world. When science became the standard trying to do the same, there evolved a great divide, what might be referred to as *mind over matter*. Traditional science centered on the study of our physical world, thus "matter". So science left "the mind" to religion. The mysteries of our minds, our consciousness, and the burning questions like "why are here?" seemed to fall under the realm of the non local or spiritual worlds.

So the opposing endeavors of science and religion went their separate ways and never the twain shall meet again–until now.

Religion and science are not mutually exclusive but represent two complementary approaches to seeking truth and understanding the nature of reality. Both religion and science share a common goal: to unravel the mysteries of existence and provide meaningful answers to life's big questions.

While religion tends to rely on faith, spiritual experiences, and ancient wisdom, science utilizes empirical evidence, observation, and the scientific method to explore the physical world. Rather than conflicting with one another, I would argue that when properly understood, religion and science can actually enrich and enhance our understanding of reality.

Acknowledging that the quantum field serves as the underlying fabric of the universe, in which everything is interconnected and interdependent, this field of pure potentiality, is where the boundaries between science and spirituality blur. It suggests that consciousness itself is a fundamental aspect of reality, and that our thoughts, intentions, and beliefs can influence the physical world. Isn't that also what faithful prayer does?

I don't think we have to choose between religion and science, but rather, we can integrate the wisdom of both.

The Science and The Spiritual

In the field of neuroscience, studies have shown that certain biomolecules in the brain, such as microtubules, exhibit quantum behavior and may play a role in our conscious experience. This connection between quantum physics and consciousness aligns with the concept of Divine Intelligence, as it suggests that our thoughts, emotions, and self-awareness are intertwined with a higher cosmic intelligence.

The phenomenon of synchronicity, coined by psychologist Carl Jung, refers to meaningful coincidences that occur in our lives, seemingly unrelated events that hold significance and purpose. Quantum physics offers an explanation for this phenomena through its principles of non-locality and interconnectedness. Similarly, Divine Intelligence suggests that these synchronicities are not mere chance but orchestrated moments of guidance and interconnectedness from a higher source or God.

In quantum physics, the observer effect demonstrates that our thoughts and intentions can influence the behavior of particles on a quantum level. Similarly, the concept of prayer and intention in spiritual traditions suggests that our focused thoughts and desires can influence the flow of Divine Intelligence, bringing about desired outcomes. Both perspectives recognize the power of conscious intention in shaping our reality.

Near-death experiences (NDEs) provide another intriguing example that combines the quantum field and Divine Intelligence. NDEs are often described as deeply spiritual and transformative encounters with a divine presence or higher intelligence. Some researchers propose that these experiences could be a result of the brain entering a heightened quantum state, allowing for a direct connection to the quantum field and Divine Intelligence. The profound life-changing effects and shared characteristics of NDEs parallel the notions of transcendent experiences and encounters with higher realms described in spiritual traditions.

The Baha'i Faith

The Baha'i Faith holds the delicate interplay between two great forces, science and religion, in the highest regard. In fact, it firmly believes that both religion and science are essential pathways to understanding the truth of our existence and are in complete harmony with one another.

The Baha'i Writings teach us that religion and science are like two wings on which humankind can soar to the heights of knowledge and understanding. They are not opposing forces, but rather complementary aspects of a greater truth. This is a refreshing stance that distinguishes the Baha'i Faith from many other religions and positions it as a true champion of intellectual curiosity and scientific exploration.

Baha'u'llah, the founder of the Baha'i Faith, emphatically declared that religion must be in harmony with science and reason. The Baha'i Faith teaches that religion, without science, soon degenerates into superstition and fanaticism, while science without religion becomes merely the instrument of crude materialism.

The Bahai writings say: "*When religion is upheld by science and reason we can believe with assurance and act with conviction, for this rational faculty is the greatest power in the world. Through it, industries are established, the past and present are laid bare and the underlying realities are brought to light. Let us make nature our captive, break through all laws of limitation and with deep penetration bring to light that which is hidden.*"

These words, my dear reader, represent the very essence of how the Baha'i Faith views the relationship between religion and science. Baha'i writings also make clear, "*God has endowed man with intelligence and reason whereby he is required to determine the verity of questions and propositions. If religious beliefs and opinions are found contrary to the standards of science they are mere superstitions and imaginations; for the antithesis of knowledge is ignorance, and the child of ignorance is superstition. Unquestionably there must be agreement between true religion and science.*"

Baha'is believe that religion and science should not only agree but should inform and inspire one another. Science, with its systematic study and empirical approach, uncovers the mysteries of the physical world. Religion, on the other hand, delves into the realm of the spiritual and metaphysical, providing insight into the purpose and meaning of our existence. The Baha'i Faith recognizes and celebrates the distinct and valuable contributions that each domain brings to the table.

But how do we reconcile potential conflicts between science and religious dogma, you may wonder? Well, the Baha'i Faith encourages its adherents to embrace an ever-advancing civilization of knowledge, where scientific discoveries are embraced and integrated into our understanding of the world. Baha'is are called upon to independently investigate the truth and not blindly adhere to outdated beliefs or uninformed interpretations of sacred texts. They are encouraged to explore the harmony between scientific discoveries and the spiritual teachings of the Faith.

It is important to note that the Baha'i Writings do not claim to provide scientific explanations for every physical phenomenon. Rather, they offer a framework for understanding the spiritual reality that lies beyond the grasp of scientific inquiry. Like the light of the sun that illuminates the world, science shines its rays on the physical plane, while religion illuminates the realm of the spirit. Together, they cast a radiant glow of understanding that enhances our appreciation for the complexity and beauty of both the seen and unseen realms.

Chapter 19

Prayer and Manifestation: Interwoven Threads Of Divine Synchronicity

"The universe conspires with us when we follow our purpose." - Paulo Coelho

Prayer and Faith

Prayer is undeniably connected to manifestation. Prayer, at its core, is an act of communication with a higher power, a way to express our desires, hopes, and dreams. It has long been believed that through prayer, we can attract positive outcomes, blessings, and tangible changes in our lives. This is also the promise of manifesting.

Faith is complete trust or confidence in someone or something. Religious or spiritual faith gives believers the unwavering credence that they are aligned with God or the Divine Source. This kind of faith sets spiritual people apart from non-believers or those who can not consciously accept that there is a God or a higher power. Spiritual people and those following a certain religious doctrine trust and are confident in the truth of God or the Divine Source, based on their spiritual conviction rather than proof.

Faith aligned with one's prayers, can be correlated to the process in manifesting where one must believe with certainty that their said desire will become manifest; that in fact it already exists and will come to be. But having faith that your prayers will be answered can be a bit nuanced. I grew up Christian, and back in those days, there was no promise you would get what you prayed for.

In my religious upbringing it was quite common to resort to the fact that sometimes God says "no" to our prayers. For some, no matter how hard they pray, things don't always pan out. And for many, these disappointments turn into a resignation that God always knows best or it's all up to God to grant our wishes as He sees fit; within Him lies all power and followers of religion do not have access to His power. We must instead supplicate earnestly and humbly, accepting the outcome we get.

However, over the years, I have witnessed a transformation in today's religious communities. Progressive Christian communities are kinder, gentler, and focused on the command "to love one another". They take the Bible seriously, but not necessarily literally, embracing reason, instead of blind allegiance to rigid dogmas. And prayer now-a-days is filled with gratitude and a "knowing" that if a prayer seems unanswered, then well, that is the answer.

In other words, there is a trust that you will get what you want when the time is right. And this is similar to the art of Manifestation which affirms your desire will be made manifest in a way and in a timeline that will be manipulated just for you in a perfect way that is perfect just for you. Sometimes we don't get the outcome we tried to manifest, but instead end up getting a better version of our desires, something we didn't ever realize we wanted, but exactly what we truly needed.

Religion and Manifestation

Throughout various world religions, the concept of prayer has been integral to connecting with the divine and manifesting desired outcomes in life. When we explore different world religions, we find striking parallels between their teachings and the concept of manifestation.

For example, in Christianity, Jesus emphasized the importance of faith in prayer and He had the ability to manifest miracles. In Buddhism, the practice of mindfulness and meditation cultivates a state of awareness and clarity that enhances manifestation. Islamic traditions encourage believers to pray with intention and trust in the power of Allah's guidance and manifestations of your supplications.

I clearly remember passages from the Bible saying, *"Seek and ye shall find, knock and the door will be opened, ask and it shall be given unto you"*. In Christianity, the Bible also teaches that *"whatever you ask for in prayer, believe that you have received it and it will be yours"*. This aligns with the core principles of manifestation, which emphasize the importance of holding unwavering belief and faith in our desired outcomes.

In Hinduism, the law of karma suggests that our thoughts, intentions, and actions directly shape our reality. In Sanskrit, *karma* literally means "action", all kinds of action, action intended, and unintended action on mental, physical, emotional and spiritual levels. In Hindu, Jain, Sikh and Buddhist philosophies, *karma* denotes the cycle of cause and effect. Like causes produce similar effects. For instance, right actions produce good results while wrong actions produce bad ones. This concept closely resembles the idea that the energy we emit through prayer or manifestation will be reciprocated by the universe, influencing the outcomes we experience.

Just as Christianity has modernized, so have ideas about karma and as a spokesperson for a new deeper understanding of karma, Deepak Chopra suggests that every action generates a force of energy that returns to us in like kind. In other words, "what we sow is what we reap". He explains, when we choose actions that bring happiness and success to others, the fruit of our karma is happiness and success.

However, Chopra dissects the idea of karma to reveal a more sophisticated way of looking at it. When we make choices, we need to witness them by bringing them into our conscious awareness. We need to ask ourselves what are the consequences of this choice and will it bring fulfillment to me and those who might be affected by this choice. If a choice feels comfortable, I will visualize how things might go, in order to make certain that I am aware of its effect on others.

This model of karma resembles the art of manifestation where if you know what you want, ask for it, and behave as if it is coming, then it will come. But by relying on our inner vision, if something does not manifest, that situation might simply be a sign for us to course-correct. Our past karma is what has made us who we are, and while we may not be perfect, karma is also about undoing what does not serve us so we can become who we really are and move forward toward our higher purpose.

In this light, karma is not so much a cycle of causes and effects, it is about action. Karma is a philosophy of how to live our lives so we can truly become the best version of ourselves and live the life we desire. We can change the path of our life by our thoughts and the choices we make. Because everything is energy, we are energy in motion and everything we do creates a corresponding energy that comes back to us.

The practice of mindfulness and meditation allows individuals to cultivate focus, clarity, and intention. This heightened state of consciousness is integral to both prayer and manifestation, as it helps us direct our thoughts and energies towards our desired goals.

Through the lens of religion and ancient spiritual practices, we not only gain insight into the age-old practice of prayer but also discover how it aligns with the principles of manifestation.

Science and Prayer

There is a profound relationship between prayer and manifestation, undoubtedly. And in recent years, scientific studies have dipped into the spiritual realms of our existence, shedding some light on the powerful effects of prayer and other spiritual phenomena and its correlation to manifestation.

From a psychological standpoint, prayer can be seen as a form of positive affirmation and visualization. When we pray, we focus our thoughts and emotions on a specific intention or outcome, similar to how manifestation emphasizes the power of positive thoughts and emotions. By aligning our conscious and subconscious mind with our desires through prayer, we open ourselves up to receive and manifest those desires in our lives.

Neuroscience has also made significant strides in understanding the connection between prayer and manifestation. Studies have shown that prayer activates certain areas of the brain associated with positive emotions, hope, and gratitude. These neurobiological changes contribute to an increased sense of well-being and a heightened state of receptivity, which are essential for effective manifestation. Modern scientific discoveries in neuroscience provide evidence for the neurological benefits of prayer and how it can impact our ability to manifest our desires.

There are a number of scientific studies on the efficacy of prayer and manifestation. For example, studies conducted by Dr. Herbert Benson at Harvard Medical School discovered that during prayer or meditation, our brainwaves shift into a state of deep relaxation and heightened receptivity, stimulating the release of beneficial neurochemicals and promoting overall well-being.

In the field of quantum physics, the observer effect suggests that our thoughts and intentions have a profound impact on the vibrational energy of the universe. When one prays they are in effect "observing", focusing on the thing that they are praying for. This act of observing collapses the waves of possibility in particles of matter, into the physical world. With both prayer and manifestation, we are essentially influencing the quantum field and allowing for the manifestation of our desires.

Divine synchronicity, according to Deepak Chopra, is the interconnectedness and meaningful coincidences that occur in our lives when we align ourselves with the divine flow of the universe. It is the beautiful dance between our intentions, desires, and the unfolding of events in perfect harmony. Synchronicity is not mere chance or luck; it is a manifestation of the unseen forces at work in the cosmos.

To fully grasp the concept of divine synchronicity, we must understand that everything in the universe is interconnected. Each person, event, and circumstance holds a unique place in the grand tapestry of existence. When we tap into this interconnectedness through our thoughts, emotions, and actions, we open ourselves to the flow of divine synchronicity.

Manifestation, One Step Beyond Prayer

Manifesting is more than just praying in the traditional sense. While prayer is an essential aspect of manifesting, it is not the sole factor. Prayer is a way to connect with the divine, to express our gratitude, to humble ourselves before the seat of God, the Divine Source of all things, to ask for assistance, heal the sick, give light and love to the downtrodden and to ask that our wants, needs, and wishes be met. It is through our sincere prayers that we establish a conscious relationship with God, the higher power or universal intelligence.

Manifesting goes beyond prayer as it involves aligning our thoughts, beliefs, and actions with those intentions. It is incumbent on our belief that what we have asked for will undoubtedly be given. It requires us to acknowledge that it already has been received. In manifesting we co-create our reality as active participants instead of waiting for "the creator" or God to grant us our wish.

It's important to understand that manifesting is not about controlling or manipulating outcomes. It is about surrendering to the divine flow and trusting that the universe knows what is best for us. In this sense it does also tie in with the aspect of prayers being inline with what God may want for us.

Are you open enough to accept that God is synonymous with the Quantum Field, or the Universe, or the Divine Intelligence, or the Source Energy, or whatever name you use, and that prayer is synonymous with manifesting? I believe this is all perhaps a part of our evolution of spiritual understanding. These ideas will be explored and examined in much greater detail in another philosophical book I am working on and hope to publish soon.

Manifesting is a creative process where we engage with the Divine Intelligence and its universal energies and draw that energy towards us. It involves visualizing our desires, believing in limitless possibilities, and taking inspired action towards them. This process is fueled by cultivating a mindset of gratitude and unwavering faith.

Coincidences and Synchronicity

"Coincidence is God's way of remaining anonymous." - Albert Einstein

Divine Synchronicity, according to Deepak Chopra, can be defined as the mystical phenomenon of meaningful coincidences that happen in our lives. These synchronicities are not mere chance occurrences but rather purposeful connections that are orchestrated by a higher power, guiding us along our journey.

The universe is not random but rather, interconnected, and everything in our lives is imbued with meaning and significance. Divine synchronicity is a way for the universe to communicate with us, offering guidance and support on our path.

Divine synchronicity is not limited to grand or life-changing events but can also manifest in everyday occurrences. It can be experienced through encounters with people who seem to appear at just the right time, unexpected opportunities that align perfectly with our desires and aspirations, or even through signs and symbols that provide clarity and direction.

To fully understand and harness the power of divine synchronicity, one must cultivate a state of awareness and live each moment, being present in the moment. This heightened level of consciousness allows us to recognize and appreciate the synchronicities that occur in our lives, making us more receptive to their messages. By paying attention to the subtle signs and connections that arise, we can begin to trust in the underlying order and intelligence of the universe.

Divine synchronicity is a tool for personal transformation and growth. By being open and receptive to the synchronicities that occur, we can tap into a greater sense of purpose and meaning in our lives. These synchronicities can guide us towards opportunities and experiences that align with our deepest desires, helping us to manifest abundance and fulfillment.

If you believe in divine synchronicity, meaningful coincidences will happen more often and with greater and greater significance. Allowing yourself to go with the flow of the universe each day, will turn your life into a dance of intentions, desires, and perfectly orchestrated unfolding events.

JOURNAL AND WORKBOOK ACTIVITIES

The 12 laws of karma can help you understand how karma really works and how to create good karma in your life.

- Examine these laws, and copy them into your journal.
- Reflect upon the laws that speak to you.
- Make a note of which ones you need to develop more.
- Make a note of which ones are already a part of your life.

1. The law of cause and effect
   According to this law, whatever thoughts or energy you put out, you get back, good or bad.

2. The law of creation
   Ask yourself what you need to release so you can create space for the thing you desire.

3. The law of humility
   Accept that you created this reality by not performing as well as you could have in the past.

4. The law of growth
   Real change or personal growth begins with what you have control over, which is yourself, not others. Your growth is dependent on you.

5. The law of responsibility
   You are the product of the choices you make.

6. The law of connection
   Everything in your life, including your past, present, and future, are connected.

7. The law of focus
   Concentrate on one thing at a time.

8. The law of giving and hospitality
   You must give to the things you believe in. Understand the importance of your actions. This should reflect your deeper beliefs.

9. The law of here and now
   Embrace the present. Let go of negative thoughts from your past.

10. The law of change
    History will continue to repeat itself until you learn from the experience and take steps to do something differently to stop the cycle.

11. The law of patience and reward
    Be consistent in your karmic deeds each and every day. Believe you can achieve your goals and trust in time they will come to fruition.

12. The law of significance and inspiration
    Every contribution you make will affect the world. What we share may sometimes seem small to us but can make an enormous difference in someone else's life. You have been born with a specific gift, mission, and purpose that only you can bring into the world with your uniqueness. Authentically sharing your skills and gifts is why you're here.

Chapter 20

The Manifestation Ripple: Inspiring Others and Collective Creation

"If you want to go fast, go alone. If you want to go far, go together." - African Proverb

Collective Creation

Throughout history, we have witnessed countless examples of ordinary people coming together to achieve extraordinary feats. These instances of collective creation not only demonstrate the indomitable human spirit but also serve as a testament to the profound impact that can be achieved by uniting under a common purpose.

One such remarkable example of collective creation can be found in the suffrage movement of the late 19th and early 20th centuries. At a time when women were denied the right to vote, courageous individuals from different walks of life joined forces to challenge the status quo. These women, with their unwavering determination, organized protests, rallies, and hunger strikes, demanding their voices be heard. Led by pioneers like Susan B.

Anthony and Elizabeth Cady Stanton, they paved the way for the eventual ratification of the 19th Amendment, granting women the right to vote in the United States. This triumph of collective creation forever transformed the social, political, and economic landscape, empowering women in unimaginable ways.

Another example that stands as a testament to the extraordinary power of collective creation can be found in the civil rights movement of the 1950s and 1960s. In the face of unimaginable adversity, African Americans and their allies united in a relentless pursuit of equality and justice. Led by inspirational figures such as Martin Luther King Jr., Rosa Parks, and Malcolm X, they organized peaceful protests, sit-ins, and freedom rides, demanding an end to racial segregation and discrimination. Their collective efforts and unwavering commitment ultimately led to landmark victories, including the Civil Rights Act of 1964 and the Voting Rights Act of 1965. These pivotal moments in history marked a turning point, transforming racial relations and securing fundamental rights for all Americans.

Moving beyond the realms of social movements, we find examples of collective creation in the world of science and innovation. Take, for instance, the creation of the internet. Developed through collaborative efforts between brilliant minds from around the globe, this groundbreaking invention has revolutionized the way we communicate, work, and access information. Without the collective vision, hard work, and collaborative spirit of scientists, engineers, and thinkers, we might not have enjoyed the seamless connectivity that defines our modern world today. Or more likely, it may have manifested on a different timeline, and not as soon as it did.

History is replete with shining examples of people harnessing the power of collective creation to effect profound change. These extraordinary achievements are a testament to what can be accomplished when people come together with a shared purpose.

You have the power to manifest for others, change lives, and even change the world. The art of collective creation is a profound ability that enables us to harness the energy of our intentions and manifest positive outcomes for people beyond ourselves.

Imagine if we were all able to create a ripple effect of positive change in the lives of our loved ones and communities. This is not only possible, but it is within your reach. By understanding the principles of manifestation, honing your skills, and channeling your intent with focus and clarity, you too can become a catalyst for transformation.

Collective creation is the awe-inspiring process of coming together with others to manifest a shared vision or intention into reality. It is the power of individuals joining forces, pooling their diverse talents, skills, and perspectives, and working collaboratively towards a common goal.

Imagine a group of passionate individuals, driven by a shared purpose, uniting their energies and talents to create something far greater than what any single person could achieve alone. It is a synergy, where the whole becomes greater than the sum of its parts.

Collective creation is not just about collaboration; it goes beyond mere teamwork. It taps into the unlimited potential of human connection and fosters an environment where everyone's unique contributions are valued and harnessed to their fullest extent.

In this collective space, boundaries are dissolved, and innovation flourishes. People inspire each other, challenge each other, and push the boundaries of what is possible. It is a space of immense creativity, where ideas are freely shared, expanded upon, refined, and brought to life.

To truly understand the power of collective creation, let me share a story with you. Picture a group of passionate women who are determined to address the issue of food insecurity in their community. Instead of embarking on individual efforts, they decide to come together and create a community garden.

Through collective creation, each woman brings her unique skills to the table. One member offers her gardening expertise, sharing her knowledge of crop rotation and irrigation techniques. Another woman, skilled in fundraising, rallies the community to gather the necessary resources. A graphic designer creates eye-catching posters to promote the project, while a chef volunteers to teach cooking classes using the garden's produce.

The collective energy and shared commitment of these women propel the project forward. They not only grow an abundance of fresh vegetables but also create a space for learning and connection. Neighbors, inspired by their efforts, join in, offering their time and talents. As the project expands, they establish partnerships with local schools, restaurants, and neighborhood organizations, creating a sustainable ecosystem of support.

This is the essence of collective creation, a transformative force that ripples beyond the initial intention. It unleashes untapped potential, amplifies impact, and creates a sense of belonging and empowerment. Through collective creation, we have the ability to shape the world and make a difference in the lives of others.

Manifesting For Others

"Every great dream begins with a dreamer. Always remember, you have within you the strength, the patience, and the passion to reach for the stars to change the world." - Harriet Tubman

Manifestation is not a solitary endeavor; it is a collective and interconnected process. We are all connected energetically, and our thoughts, intentions, and actions can have a ripple effect, reaching far beyond ourselves. By harnessing this power, we can actively contribute to the well-being and transformation of those around us. The power to manifest and create positive change is not limited to oneself. As individuals, we possess incredible potential to influence and impact the lives of others and even make a difference on a global scale.

To manifest for others, it's essential to understand the underlying principles and mechanisms at work. Firstly, it's crucial to align your intention with the highest good and the well-being of the person you wish to help. Your intentions must be pure, selfless, and rooted in love and compassion.

When it comes to manifesting for others, it's important to remember that the foundation lies in genuine care and empathy. We must have the best interest of others at heart and seek to enhance their well-being, rather than impose our desires upon them. It's about co-creating with them, supporting their dreams, and empowering them to step into their own manifestation abilities.

One powerful way to manifest for others is through visualization and positive intention. By visualizing the desired outcome for someone else in vivid detail, you can send a surge of focused energy towards their aspirations. For example, if you want to help a friend achieve career success, imagine them confidently excelling in their chosen field, surrounded by supportive colleagues and enjoying abundance in their professional life. The power of your intention combined with their own efforts can synergistically enhance their chances of success.

Next, focus your energy and attention on visualizing the desired outcome. Envision the person's life transformed, or the world changed for the better, with as much detail as possible. Feel the emotions associated with this vision and believe wholeheartedly in its manifestation. Your belief and faith are potent catalysts for change.

Once you have set your intention and visualized the desired outcome, take inspired action. Be proactive in finding ways to contribute towards the change you seek. Whether it's offering support, sharing knowledge, or actively participating in initiatives or organizations that align with your vision, your actions will amplify and reinforce your intentions.

Another way to manifest for others is through the practice of affirmation and positive reinforcement. Offer sincere words of encouragement and support towards their goals and dreams. Affirmations have the ability to shift one's mindset, raise self-belief, and pave the way for the manifestation of their desires. By consistently reinforcing their positive qualities and capabilities, you uplift their spirits and create a fertile ground for transformation.

In terms of changing lives and even the world, the key lies in starting small and expanding your impact gradually. Touching the lives of a few individuals with your positive intentions and actions can create a ripple effect that spreads far and wide. By focusing on making a difference in the lives of those around you, you become a beacon of inspiration for others to follow.

However, it's important to acknowledge that while we can influence and support the manifestation process for others, everyone has their own free will and personal journey. It's important to respect the autonomy and free will of others. Manipulating or controlling someone's life without their consent goes against the principles of manifestation.

We cannot force outcomes or manipulate others to fit our desires. Instead, focus on offering positive energy, guidance, and support when needed, empowering others to unlock their own potential. Manifesting for others is about providing the love, support, and positive energy needed for them to unlock their own potential.

Manifesting for others, changing lives, and even changing the world is not only possible but also a responsibility we should embrace. By mastering the principles of collective creation, offering genuine support, and channeling our intentions with love and clarity, we have the power to inspire and empower those around us to live their best lives and create a positive impact in the world.

Manifesting for others may not happen overnight. It requires consistency, patience, resilience, and unwavering belief in the power of your intentions. The results may unfold gradually, revealing the impact of your efforts over time. Trust in the timing of the universe and continue to persevere in your mission.

Research and numerous studies have shown that positive energy, thoughts, and intentions create a tangible and measurable impact on individuals and the world as a whole. The power of collective consciousness can be a force for monumental change. So, embrace your role as a catalyst for transformation, and go forth with enthusiasm, precision, and unwavering determination to manifest for others, change lives, and or ultimately change the world.

> *"Individually, we are one drop. Together, we are an ocean." - Ryunosuke Satoro*

So, to all who are curious about unlocking the secret to living in abundance, let us draw inspiration from those who have made a difference through collective creation and embrace the potential that lies within. The time is now, and the possibilities are boundless.

Let us seize this opportunity to embark on our own journey of manifesting, manifesting for others, and even collective creation, so as to make a lasting impact on our world, just as those before us have done. You have the power and ability to shape a future that is boldly and beautifully your own.

JOURNAL AND WORKBOOK ACTIVITIES

- What is something that you would like to change or bring into being in your community of family, or friends, in your neighborhood, city, or your child's school? It might be a state issue, a national issue, or it could be centered on social, political, economic issues, whatever. Search your heart and explore the idea of working with others to manifest something that would benefit not only yourself but others.

- Jot down as many ideas as you can think of in your journal. You don't have to get started on this right away, but put some thought into it. Who knows what the future will bring to your attention, but right now is as good enough time as any, to contemplate a possible course of action to carry out when the timing is right.

- After completing your brainstorming session, answer the following questions to test the fidelity of your ideas for a possible collective creation, manifesting along with others for the common good.

1. Intentions:
   Are your intentions pure, selfless, and rooted in love and compassion?
   Are you aligning your intention with the highest good and well-being of the person or the world you wish to help?

2. Visualization:
   Are you visualizing the desired outcome with as much detail as possible?
   Are you feeling the emotions associated with this vision and believing wholeheartedly in its manifestation?

3. Action:
   Are you taking inspired action to contribute towards the change you seek?
   Are you actively finding ways to support, share knowledge, or participate in initiatives or organizations aligned with your vision?

4. Respect:
   Are you respecting individual free will and autonomy in your manifestation process?
   Are you offering positive energy, guidance, and support without manipulation or control?

5. Consistency and Patience:
   Are you consistently maintaining your intentions and actions over time?
   Are you practicing patience, resilience, and unwavering belief in the power of your intentions?

6. Trust in Timing:
   Are you trusting in the timing of the universe and its unfolding of results?
   Are you persevering in your mission despite gradual or delayed outcomes?

7. Impact:
   Are you aware of the tangible and measurable impact that positive energy, thoughts, and intentions can have on individuals and the world as a whole?
   Are you embracing your role as a catalyst for transformation with enthusiasm, precision, and unwavering determination?

Chapter 21

Together Strong: The Empowerment of a Supportive Community

"The greatness of a community is most accurately measured by the compassionate actions of its members." - Coretta Scott King

If you find yourself buying into the ideas presented in this book or the overwhelming compilation of science and quantum physics that back it up or if you've always been intrigued by the idea of manifestation or even if you are an expert in manifesting already, belonging to a supportive community that values and believes in the power of manifestation is essential for several key reasons.

Firstly, such a community provides a nurturing environment that fosters personal growth and empowerment. When individuals come together with shared beliefs and goals, their collective energy and enthusiasm become a powerful force for positive change. This sense of belonging and collaboration strengthens one's motivation and determination to manifest their desires.

Secondly, being part of a supportive community allows individuals to learn from and lean on like-minded people who have experience and knowledge in manifesting their dreams. The exchange of ideas, tips, and strategies within this community can be immensely valuable in accelerating personal growth and manifestation abilities. By surrounding yourself with individuals who have successfully manifested their desires, you can gain insights and inspiration, ultimately enhancing your own manifestation journey.

Moreover, belonging to a supportive community helps to break free from limiting beliefs and societal conditioning. Being surrounded by individuals who genuinely believe in the power of manifestation can encourage you to step out of your comfort zone and challenge any doubts or skepticism you may have. This community acts as a constant reminder that you are not alone in your beliefs, giving you the confidence to embrace the magic of manifestation and manifest limitless possibilities in your life.

Furthermore, a supportive community provides a safe space for individuals to share their manifestations, successes, and challenges. Celebrating achievements together amplifies the sense of joy and fulfillment, while also inspiring others to believe in their own manifestation abilities. Additionally, when facing obstacles or setbacks, having a supportive network offers solace, guidance, and encouragement, empowering individuals to stay motivated and focused on their goals.

Last but not least, scientific research supports the positive impact of belonging to a supportive community on overall well-being and success. Studies have shown that individuals with strong social support systems have higher levels of resilience, self-esteem, and life satisfaction. This not only enhances their manifestation abilities but also contributes to their overall happiness and fulfillment in life.

In conclusion, belonging to a supportive community that values and believes in the power of manifestation is vital for personal growth, learning, overcoming limiting beliefs, and staying motivated on the manifestation journey. The collective energy, wisdom, and encouragement within such a community create a powerful environment for individuals to thrive and manifest their dreams. So, if you are curious about the secret to living your best life and want to align yourself with like-minded people who can support and inspire you, joining a supportive manifestation community is the empowering choice you should make.

JOURNAL AND WORKBOOK ACTIVITIES

Visit my website at freakflagfun.com for more information on a WOMEN EMPOWERING WOMEN platform that I am currently developing. It promises to be a unique combination of courses for personal growth and manifestation along with a social network of support to connect you with like minded women around the world, ready to support you, challenge you, connect with you, hear your ideas, cheer you on, and ultimately make us all better people living lives of abundance and inspiring others to do the same!

-Kristina Perdue

FIND YOUR PEOPLE! BE COURAGEOUS! SHARE YOUR TRUTH!

1. Nurture Personal Growth: Ensure that you are actively engaging in self-reflection and personal development activities to foster your own growth.

2. Embrace Collaboration: Seek out opportunities to collaborate with others to harness collective energy and enthusiasm for positive change.

3. Learn from Others: Take advantage of the knowledge and experience of like-minded individuals by actively participating in discussions and sharing ideas, tips, and strategies.

4. Challenge Limiting Beliefs: Continuously challenge any doubts or skepticism you may have by actively engaging with those who embrace their belief in the power of manifestation.

5. Celebrate Achievements: Share your manifestations,

successes, and challenges with others to celebrate achieve-ments and stay motivated on your manifestation journey.

6. Lean on Community for Support: When facing obstacles or setbacks, seek solace, guidance, and encouragement from supportive networks to maintain motivation and focus on your goals.

7. Prioritize Well-being: Recognize the positive impact that belonging to a supportive community can have on your overall well-being and success. Prioritize staying connected and engaged with the community to maintain high levels of resilience, self-esteem, and life satisfaction.

Chapter 22

Hologram Hypothesis: Are We Living in a Holographic Universe?

"Everything we call real is made of things that cannot be regarded as real." - Niels Bohr

I chose to end with this chapter because if there are any of my readers who still think manifesting is just too far fetched to believe in, well, this is maybe bigger than that. What I'm about to share with you most likely doesn't come up on your TikTok or Instagram feed.

The amazing minds of world renowned theoretical physicists are currently researching the idea of the Hologram Hypothesis using mathematical proofs, arguably the most effective quantitative language we have for the sciences. At any rate, science, physics, astronomy, geometry, quantum mechanics, and math are all pointing toward something remarkable and a bit difficult to swallow.

Imagine, for a moment, that everything we perceive as reality is just a projection, a three-dimensional illusion created by a two-dimensional surface, where information is not distributed throughout space, but rather encoded onto a flat surface.

Yes, you heard that right: a universe that may, in fact, be a colossal cosmic hologram! It sounds like something out of a sci-fi movie, but the evidence supporting this theory is truly compelling.

To illustrate this, imagine being inside a vast, empty theater. The large screen in this theater is the reality of our world. This ultra-high-definition screen is covered in a limitless array of pixels. These pixels, infinitesimally small and arranged in a precise pattern, contain all the information about the objects and particles within our reality. It's as if every single bit of our universe is projected onto this mysterious holographic surface, and we are merely players within its grand cosmic theater.

Now, you may be thinking, "But how can this mind-bending idea possibly be true?" Well that is where the true beauty of the Holographic Universe lies. The concept of living in a holographic universe is an awe-inspiring idea that has been gaining traction in the scientific community. While it may seem far-fetched at first glance, the mounting evidence and the profound implications of this theory make it a subject worth exploring further.

First proposed by Gerard 't Hooft and soon built upon by others, a groundbreaking theory known as the Holographic Principle was introduced to the scientific community. According to this principle, all the information and physical properties of our universe, electromagnetism, and the behavior of particles, including the properties of gravity, can be encoded on a two-dimensional surface. This surface is sometimes referred to as a "holographic screen" or "boundary."

In other words, everything we experience in our three-dimensional world may be a projection or a holographic representation of the information stored on this two-dimensional surface.

Juan Maldacena of the Institute for Advanced Study in Princeton, New Jersey added to the ideas in this principle when he put forth a conjecture that shook the world of theoretical physics. He posits that our universe, with all its dimensions, forces, and matter, can be mathematically described by a simpler theory that exists on the boundary of the universe. This simpler theory is essentially a hologram, a projection of the information inside our universe.

Using the ideas behind string theory, Maldacena found two different theories that could describe the same physical system, showing that the theories were equivalent, even though one factored in gravity and the other didn't.

This is big. Because in physics the idea of "gravity" has been the stumbling block in connecting quantum physics to the theory of relativity.

But the duality of Maldacena's theory has largely held up. It argues that we can understand what happens inside a volume of spacetime that has gravity by studying the quantum-mechanical behavior of particles and fields at that volume's surface, using a theory with one less dimension, one in which gravity plays no role.

Physicists have repeatedly tested this theory's efficacy and have used it to continue the search for the missing link involving gravity. In the 1970's Stephen Hawking used this holographic theory to learn more about black holes.

The evidence supporting the holographic universe theory is compelling. One of the most fascinating clues comes from black holes, those cosmic enigmas that devour light and matter. Stephen Hawking himself made a groundbreaking discovery, showing that the entropy, or the amount of disorder, of a black hole is proportional to the surface area of its event horizon, rather than its volume. This "surface area-law" is consistent with the holographic principle, suggesting that the information inside a black hole can be described by the physics on its boundary.

Furthermore, scientists have observed bizarre connections between black holes and quantum entanglement, a phenomenon where particles become mysteriously linked, regardless of the distance between them. Recent research has shown that the mathematics of entanglement can be beautifully explained by the holographic principle. It appears that the entanglement patterns between particles are mirrored by the geometric patterns on the holographic screen, further strengthening the idea that our reality is a holographic projection.

And Hawking's discoveries enabled others to connect the entanglement entropy of the quantum system to the surface of a black hole.

Since then numerous theories, too complicated to recount here, have built upon each other and at this point in time, physicists hope that these insights will get them to a theory of quantum gravity for our own universe. The community is working hard and many of these theoretical physicists are optimistic.

The current trend of understanding puts forth that while we used to think the physical universe was composed of matter and energy, physicists now speculate and suggest that the physical world is made up of information, with energy and matter as incidentals.

To grasp this concept, let's imagine a hologram of a rose. When we shine light through the hologram, a stunning three-dimensional image of a rose appears before our eyes, seemingly floating in mid-air. However, if we were to slice the hologram into smaller pieces, each individual piece would still contain the entire image of the rose, just at a lower resolution.

This property of holography, where a part contains the whole, is the fundamental idea behind the Holographic Principle. Is it possible then to see the world in a grain of sand?

If it turns out that our own universe has some underlying holographic description, it would be as big of a leap in our understanding of the universe as anything else that's happened before in the history of physics.

You see, if this theory holds up, it suggests that our perceived reality is not as solid and fixed as it seems. Rather, it implies that everything, from the tiniest subatomic particle to the vast expanse of intergalactic space, is nothing more than a projection of information encoded on this holographic surface. It ignites the realization that we are not separate from the universe but deeply interconnected, like strands of an intricate cosmic tapestry.

Now, you might wonder how this mind-boggling theory could possibly enhance our understanding of ourselves. Well, the holographic universe concept holds the potential to revolutionize our thinking about consciousness, perception, and the very nature of reality itself. If our universe is indeed a holographic projection, it implies that our thoughts, intentions, and beliefs may have a profound influence on the fabric of reality.

So, how can we use this knowledge? By understanding that our reality is malleable and that our thoughts and intentions can shape the very fabric of the hologram we can tap into our innate power to manifest the life we desire, to bend reality to our will.

But hold on a second, my ambitious souls, let's not get carried away in our enthusiasm. While the Holographic Universe theory is undeniably captivating, it is still a theory, and with science constantly evolving, new findings may either solidify or modify this tantalizing concept.

Nonetheless, the Holographic Universe theory reminds us of the awe-inspiring mystery that lies at the heart of our existence. It propels us to expand our minds, and perhaps, in doing so, to unlock the secrets of life.

So, what does this mean? It means that by tapping into our innate creative power, by aligning our thoughts, intentions, and actions with the surface of information that defines the holographic universe, we can use its power to attract abundance, love, and success in ways we never thought possible. By understanding that we are interconnected with everything around us, that we are part of this magnificent hologram of existence, we can grasp the immense potential within ourselves and unleash it to achieve our wildest dreams.

Chapter 23

All Science Points to Possibilities: Making the Case for Manifestation

"The only limit to our realization of tomorrow will be our doubts of today." - Franklin D. Roosevelt

As I attempt to wrap up this manuscript, I feel the need to revisit all the science I have gathered and presented to you, in an effort to help the doubters overcome this crippling shortcoming that often rears its head in the so-called rational world. I recognize and attest to the fact that some of the science is based on the research of theoretical physicists which may not be formally accepted yet by the scientific community. I also need to stress there is plenty of real science presented here that supports the art of manifestation.

Additionally, I hope I have made you more aware of the very current, groundbreaking and ongoing studies that together are shaping what will one day be tomorrow's scientific understanding for many of the mysteries that are yet to be discovered. And honestly, I just skimmed the surface of recent research. There is so much happening in science and physics today and I wish I could have included more, but that may come in another book I'd like to write defending the science pertaining to manifestation.

Let's Review

Quantum Physics. Originally referred to as Quantum Mechanics, Quantum Physics is science's most rigorously tested field of physics. Simply put it is the study of the tiniest things, like atoms and particles. It operates in the non-local world.

Particle-Wave Duality. The phenomenon asserts that everything in the universe has both a particle and a wave nature. This makes quantum physics all about probabilities and the odds are encapsulated into a mathematical entity called the wave function.

Observer Effect. Making an observation is said to collapse the wave function, destroying the superposition and forcing the object into just one of its many possible particle states, or matter.

Superposition. Quantum objects can be in two places at once and can also exist in multiple states at once.

Quantum Entanglement. Einstein dubbed this "spooky action at distance". When two particles are bound together, or entangled, and one of them is altered in some way, the other particle is instantly altered in the same way, regardless of their distance apart. This happens faster than the speed of light, something Einstein said was impossible.

Quantum Information Science. Physicists agree that non-locality is a real phenomenon and that has triggered a good deal of experimental and theoretical effort leading to the creation of a new subfield.

Quantum physics and the art of manifesting go hand in hand.

The art of manifestation takes place in the non-local realm as does quantum physics. And just as subatomic particles can exist in multiple places at once, our desires also exist in this field of possibilities. The wave-particle duality and the observer effect correlates to manifestation as we envision a desire, harness the power of intention, and then from our observation, we collapse all the possibilities into a specific outcome bringing our desire into physical reality. It is within the quantum field of energy, the field of uncertainty, the field of infinite possibilities, where manifestations of our desires can occur.

Neuroscience. The brain has the ability to send instructions to cells in our bodies producing cell growth, metabolism, our immune response, and hormonal balance. Neuroscientific research also supports the notion that focused and positive thinking can impact the brain's neural circuitry, leading to changes in behavior and outcomes.

Neuroplasticity. Scientists discovered you can literally change your brain, strengthen its abilities, and enhance cognitive function. The brain has the ability to rewire and reorganize itself, in fact, your brain can change and adapt throughout your entire life.

The art of manifestation relies on each of us to train our brains through focused thought and meditation. By training our brains to reinforce constructive thought patterns and beliefs, we can conceivably optimize our potential for manifestation. Neuroscience and the concept of neuroplasticity reveal the power of our brains to create and change, which is practically manifestation defined.

Coherence. Coherence occurs when the brain's electrical and magnetic frequencies are synchronously aligned, allowing the various brain regions to communicate seamlessly. This signifies a state of optimal brain functioning. Coherence also has a profound impact on your physiology and emotions.

Many meditations for manifesting begin with a focused effort to bring the brain into coherence using visualization and meditation techniques. With your brain in coherence, the power of your physiology and emotions are enhanced, which helps to facilitate the principle steps for manifestation.

Quantum Cognition. Quantum Cognition seeks to use the language of quantum probability to describe the way people think and behave. Quantum cognition explains that making one choice, judgement, or measurement can affect our later choices, judgments, or measurements, but these outcomes can be altered based on the order-effect. People's behavior under uncertainty differs from their behavior under certainty.

This directly correlates with the core ideas of manifestation, namely that our choices and certainty greatly influence the outcome of a manifested desire. It relates to how quantum cognition works in our brains.

The Quantum Brain. Growing evidence suggesting that the human brain may utilize quantum mechanics. One study suggests that quantum processes play a crucial role in our cognitive and conscious brain functions. Another study indicated that certain brain functions are quantum in nature, providing further evidence that quantum processes are deeply intertwined with our cognitive and conscious abilities.

The art of manifestation relies on our ability to harness the power of our brains and its quantum processes.

Everything is Energy. All things in the universe are made up of energy. Vibrational frequencies are unique patterns of energy that objects or entities emit. Each atom, each particle, has its own signature vibrational frequency. When multiple atoms come together to form matter, such as a chair or a tree, their combined vibrational frequencies create the physical object we perceive.

When practicing manifestation, our thoughts, emotions, and intentions also emit energy and possess their own unique vibrational frequencies. We ourselves are energy beings, capable of influencing our reality (manifesting) through the vibrational frequencies we emit and attract.

Wireless Energy. Nikola Tesla demonstrated the transfer of electrical energy wirelessly across space, showcasing the interconnectedness of energy and frequencies all around us.

Quanta. Max Plank introduced the concept of quanta, tiny packets of energy that underpin all electromagnetic radiation. Planck's energy equation, $E = hf$, where E represents energy and f stands for frequency, unveiled the interplay between energy and frequency.

The Theory of Relativity. Einstein's famous equation, $E = mc^2$, reveals the equivalence of energy (E) and mass (m), showing that energy can be transformed into matter and vice versa, matter can be transformed into energy. This profound understanding further emphasizes the inherent interconnectedness of energy frequencies and matter in the universe.

Electromagnetic Radiation. Hendrik Lorentz unveiled the concept of electromagnetic radiation, shedding light on the wave nature of energy and frequencies, electromagnetic fields, energy transmission, and frequency modulation.

Electromagnetic Fields. James Clerk Maxwell's equations mathematically described the behavior of electromagnetic fields, laying the groundwork for technologies like radio and telecommunications, demonstrating that energy frequencies are quantifiable and predictable.

The above mentioned scientists have given us substantial evidence supporting the science of energy and frequencies in all things. We can utilize vibrational frequencies to alter our own energy. The secret of manifestation lies in harnessing the abundant energy that surrounds us.

Epigenetics. Dr. Bruce Lipton is known for his work in the epigenetics, the study of changes in organisms caused by modification of gene expression rather than alteration of the genetic code. His research reveals that our genes are not fixed and predetermined, but rather influenced by our environment and the signals we send them.

The Power of The Mind. Dr. Joe Dispenza has extensively studied the power of the mind in influencing our reality. His research focuses on our brain's ability to form new neural connections based on our thoughts and experiences. He emphasizes the importance of cultivating focused intention, coupled with elevated emotions, to create a coherent energy for healing and transforming the direction of our lives.

Energy and Consciousness. Dr. Amit Goswami explains that at the most fundamental level of reality, everything is made up of energy and consciousness. He asserts that our thoughts and intentions can directly influence the quantum field, causing shifts in our external reality.

The researchers mentioned above present compelling studies that affirm our perceptions, beliefs, emotions, thoughts, energy fields, the power of our brains, and the influence we possess over our genes, can directly impact our biology and can enhance our ability to manifest our desires.

Color Does Not Exist. There is no such thing as color according to biology and neuroscience. We see wavelengths of light, visual processing centers in our brains decode these energy signals, and our minds then create a perception of color. Science also recognizes that early man by way of non-local communication, collectively constructed a shared perspective of color. All our other senses, hearing, smelling, tasting, and feeling roughly follow this same formula and are contingent upon our perception, so in effect there is no real sound, smell, taste, or texture to things we feel.

Manifestation is connected to how we see color. When we manifest we are choosing a perception of ourselves that we want to bring into being. We see color as a manifestation of energy and information and this, my friend, is exactly what we are doing when successfully manifesting.

Morphic Fields. Rupert Sheldrake introduced the idea of Morphic Resonance, referring to a collective memory present in all living systems and represented by Morphic Fields. These fields influence the behavior of organisms, allowing them to resonate with energy and information and to somehow communicate non-locally, across both space and time. These theories were initially rejected by the scientific community back in 1981, yet currently there is renewed interest in his research.

Manifestation involves connecting to the quantum field, a non-local realm of energy similar to Sheldrake's morphic field. Scientific theories now recognize this field of shared consciousness.

Biocommunication of Cells. In the 1960's Cleve Backster began measuring electrical responses of plants and found that plants could exhibit responses to thoughts and intentions from humans. In 1972 he isolated cells from human subjects and observed that the isolated cells exhibited electromagnetic responses relating to the emotional states of the subjects, despite being separated from the human body from which they originated. His work was also rejected by science back then, yet his ideas of bio-communication of cells and cellular consciousness is now being studied.

Cells Have Memories. Backster proposed that not only single cell organisms but also the cells of complete organisms possess a form of knowledge or perception. His research concluded in a non-local input model, suggesting a continuum of intelligent energy that fills all space. Again, the research of today is now aligning with Backter's early theories. Also, current studies on cellular memory as seen in organ transplant recipients, highlight the possibility that organs in our body have cellular memory, allowing them to retain information and react to external stimuli.

This research is extensively covered in a number of books and articles.

Cells Demand Sincere Intentions. Backster observed that cells have the ability to discriminate between genuine thoughts and those that lack sincerity. This research underscores the importance of the paramount role of sincere intention in cellular interactions and cell communication. Current research shows that sincere intentions from individuals, focused feelings of love, can influence the shape of DNA molecules. This provides support for the possibility of non-local input at the molecular level.

Cells and Non-Local Communication. Beyond linear time and three-dimensional space, thoughts function in "pre-space" serving as a representation of non-local inputs. In order for these to be transmitted and understood within the physical realm, they undergo a conversion process into symbols. This allows for the translation of thoughts into tangible forms that can be comprehended by our cells.

Manifestation relies on our consciousness and intention to influence our reality. If we consider the research that cells possess consciousness, can communicate with each other, and can also respond to our thoughts and intentions, then the cells in our bodies are not mere biological entities, but rather active participants in our conscious experience.

The Reticular Activating System. This system (RAS) is a bundle of nerves that sits in your brainstem and controls your subconscious mind. The RAS selectively amplifies certain inputs based on what it deems relevant and important to you. Once you register something as significant, it starts directing your attention toward it. Your subconscious mind can not differentiate between positive and negative, it merely operates based on the information it has received and the beliefs it has formed, however, it can also take instructions from your conscious mind making it possible for you to purposefully shape your subconscious mind.

When manifesting, your desires inevitably become programmed into your subconscious mind. Subsequently, the RAS becomes an instrument leading you toward fulfilling your manifestation. This is real science.

Sentience and Consciousness in Single Cells. There is a growing understanding among scientists that sentience may be present in all forms of life including single cells. A 2019 study explains sentience and consciousness in unicellular species as the presence of feelings, subjective states, and a primitive aware-ness of events, including internal states. Other studies building on this suggest that sentience and consciousness occurred with the first emergence of life in single cells and all subsequent species inherited their mental states and functions from this event. Human consciousness can be traced back to this single origin, with every other species carrying genetic material that codes for sentience.

Cognition-Based Evolution. A study from 2021 proposed Cognition-Based Evolution (CBE), challenging Neo-Darwinism, which says that genetic variations occur randomly and are subject to natural selection. CBE suggests that biological variation is the result of intelligent cells collectively evaluating and responding to ambiguous environmental cues. These cells engage in non-random natural genomic editing in response to epigenetic impacts and environmental stresses. According to this theory, cellular cognition is the foundation of biology and a new theory of evolution. Another study from 2022 building on theories of CBE focuses on the biomolecular mechanisms of cellular consciousness and further challenges our understanding of cellular organization.

Aligning our conscious desires with the consciousness of each of our cells magnifies our manifestation powers. In effect, you are creating what you want in your life, with your powerful conscious will, along with literally every cell in your body.

Causal Potency of Consciousness. A Study from 2023 posits that the physical theory of quantum reductionism emphasizes the causal potency of the conscious mind and its ability to affect the physical world, giving credence to the idea that our minds can truly transform our surroundings. Dr. Danko D. Georgieva explains that quantum mechanics already possesses the necessary mathematical ingredients to support a causally potent consciousness. Using quantum information theory, our conscious mind can be identified with the quantum state of our brain.

Like the art of Manifestation, this study says our conscious mind possesses free will and the capacity to choose among future courses of action made possible through the wave function collapse and disentanglement process, where one of the multiple outcomes is actualized. Understanding the role of quantum mechanics in our conscious choices and their effect on our physical reality allows us to use the transformative power of our minds to manifest our desired outcomes.

Quantum Consciousness. This concept suggests that microtubules in neurons in the brain might temporarily maintain superposition states, exhibiting quantum properties. This theory proposes that the act of measurement (observation) of these superposition states in the brain make human conscious experience possible.

This idea relates to manifestation as a part of our consciousness. When we consciously observe a desire in our minds, we can possibly tap into a superposition state that we want to manifest by utilizing the quantum properties of the limitless possibilities residing in the neurons in our brains.

Emotional Intelligence. It's a scientific fact that emotions precede thought. When emotions run high, they change the way our brains function, diminishing our cognitive abilities, decision-making powers, and even interpersonal skills. Emotional Intelligence (EI) is a concept that defines one's ability to recognize, understand and manage our own emotions and along with recognizing, understanding and influencing the emotions of others.

The bottom line is: You're the one who gets to control your emotions, so they don't control you. Emotional intelligence gives you power over your emotions, so you can call upon and enhance the positive emotions necessary to increase your manifestation powers.

Emotional Power. Emotions are created by the chemicals known as neuropeptides that are released in our bodies in response to our thoughts. These chemicals are messengers that communicate with our cells, influencing their behavior. Emotions also generate electromagnetic signals that carry a specific vibrational frequency. When we experience positive emotions, frequencies are high and it is easier to attract like frequencies.

The intensity of our emotions impact the signals we send to our cells, which positively affects the outcomes we manifest. Emotions are the fuel that drives our intentions and the frequency of our positive emotions determines our resonance with the quantum field of infinite possibilities.

When the Body Becomes the Mind. Our emotions are connected to our bodies. When we experience extreme emotions, our bodies feel it and store this information. When we remember, we actually remember how we feel because our bodies retrieve the emotions from our memory, enabling our brains to release the same chemicals from the original moment we were remembering. We actually relive it as we remember it. In essence, your body is your unconscious mind. It feels deeply. Which is why a broken heart is painful and hurts so badly.

In order for manifestation to work, you must truly feel the emotions associated with the desired outcome as if it has already come to be, teaching your body what it will feel like emotionally before your desire is made manifest. What you are actually doing is manipulating the biological functions in your body. If you do this correctly, your body, just like your mind, won't know the difference between what is real and what you have imagined.

Gratitude Research. For the past five decades there have been numerous studies on Gratitude from numerous universities and research organizations. Regularly practicing gratitude can affect your physical health with improved sleep quality, reduced risk of heart disease, lower blood pressure, reduced symptoms of chronic pain, a strengthened immune system and lower levels of depression and stress. Mental well being from cultivating gratitude leads to increased feelings of happiness, higher levels of optimism, increased positive emotions, prosocial behavior, empathy, compassion, and fostering more fulfilling relationships. Gratitude can enhance your overall psychological resilience, give you a greater sense of purpose in life, increase your life satisfaction, vitality, and overall well-being.

Gratitude is an incredibly powerful tool in the manifestation pro-cess, as it acts as a magnet for attracting abundance and creating a positive mindset. When we express gratitude for what we have, we open ourselves up to receive even more blessings. We shift our focus from lack and scarcity to abundance and possibility. The number one reason gratitude is powerful in manifesting is because gratitude is the highest form of receiving and will magnify your manifestation powers.

The Placebo Effect. The placebo effect refers to the beneficial effects experienced by individuals who are administered an inactive treatment, such as a sugar pill, with the belief that it is an actual therapeutic intervention. When people believe they are taking something that will make them better, their bodies respond accordingly. The placebo effect is an accepted phenomenon that has been investigated through rigorous scientific methodologies, employing double-blind, placebo-controlled trials, which are widely regarded as the gold standard in medical research.

Quantum Healing. Also known as Quantum Energy Healing or Quantum Medicine, Quantum Healing is a holistic approach to healing that integrates principles from quantum physics and various healing modalities, such as energy healing, meditation, visualization, intention setting, ancient spiritual wisdom, and various mind-body approaches. Quantum Healing has also found recognition in the field of quantum biology, which explores the intersection between quantum physics and biology. Research in quantum biology suggests that quantum phenomena, such as coherence and entanglement, may indeed play a role in biological processes, including healing.

Psychoneuroimmunology. The field of Psychoneuroimmunology (PNI) explores the intricate connections between the mind, the nervous system, and the immune system, demonstrating how psychological factors, like your thoughts and emotions, can influence immune system function and overall health. PNI provides a scientific foundation for understanding the mind-body connection and the potential influence of our internal states on healing processes.

We can manifest better overall health and we can manifest healing. The placebo effect, quantum healing, and PNI research, all support the idea that we can influence our physical well-being. The magic here lies in the power of belief. Our thoughts, emotions, and intentions can have a profound impact on our health and well-being. By consciously directing and influencing the energy within and around the body, a person can stimulate their own innate healing abilities to facilitate the body's natural healing mechanisms and restore optimal health.

Stellar Nucleosynthesis. Carl Sagan's belief that we are not separate from the universe but rather a part of it, and that the universe is expressing itself through us, is supported by scientific principles. The principles of conservation of energy and matter also support our unity with the universe, understanding that energy and matter cannot be created nor destroyed, but merely transformed from one form to another. Stellar nucleosynthesis, the study of stellar evolution and nucleosynthesis reveals that the elements that make up our bodies, such as carbon, oxygen, and iron, were formed within the cores of stars through nuclear reactions. This implies that the atoms and molecules that make up our bodies were once a part of stars, brought forth through immense cosmic processes. This process connects us to the cosmic origins of matter and reinforces our unity with the universe.

Manifestation is directly related to the idea of being in flow with the Universe. The oneness of humans, literally made from stardust, connects us to the universe. In manifesting, the universe is not only the cosmos, but also a reference to the quantum field where manifestation power is retrieved.

The Quantum Connection. Both the quantum field and Divine Intelligence (or the idea of God) defy the limitations of time and space and are thus non-local. The quantum field, through principles like superposition and tunneling, allows particles to exist in multiple states simultaneously and traverse through barriers without physical contact. In a similar vein, Divine Intelligence is believed to transcend the confines of time and space, operating beyond our human comprehension of reality. Philosophical discourse emerging by thought leaders in this arena supports the connections between the quantum field and Divine Intelligence.

Manifestation mirrors the practice of prayer. Similarly, the parallels and shared characteristics between quantum physics and Divine Intelligence present a compelling argument for the existence of a greater universal intelligence aligned with the quantum field.

Science, Prayer, and Manifestation. In recent years, scientific studies have dipped into the spiritual realms of our existence. There are a number of studies on the efficacy of prayer and meditation. A study from Harvard Medical School discovered that during prayer or meditation, our brainwaves shift into a state of deep relaxation and heightened receptivity, stimulating the release of beneficial neurochemicals and promoting overall well-being. Neuroscience studies have shown that prayer activates certain areas of the brain associated with positive emotions, hope, and gratitude. These neurobiological changes contribute to an increased sense of well-being and a heightened state of receptivity.

Manifestation and prayer share a profound relationship. By aligning our conscious and subconscious mind with our desires through prayer, we open ourselves up to receive and manifest those desires in our lives. When we pray, we focus our thoughts and emotions on a specific intention or outcome, similar to how manifestation emphasizes the power of positive thoughts and emotions.

Religion and Science Must be in Unity

"God has endowed man with intelligence and reason whereby he is required to determine the verity of questions and propositions. If religious beliefs and opinions are found contrary to the standards of science they are mere superstitions and imaginations; for the antithesis of knowledge is ignorance, and the child of ignorance is superstition. Unquestionably there must be agreement between true religion and science." -Baha'i Writings

The Wrap-Up

Taking into account all the trends and patterns in the science I have presented should give you an overview of what we've learned and how it fits together to support the ideas of manifestation. I've grouped them into categories for this purpose.

Non-local elements pertaining to the Human Experience:

Emotions, Thoughts, Intentions, Consciousness, the Mind, the Brain, Gratitude, Positive Mind-set, Emotional Intelligence, the Subconscious Mind, the Reticular Activating System, Quantum Consciousness, Casual Potency of Consciousness, Consciousness and Energy, Quantum Cognition, the Quantum Brain, Brainwaves

Non-local elements pertaining to the Human Body:

Bio-communication of Cells, Cell Memory, Sentience and Consciousness in Signal Cells, Cells and Non-local Communication, Cells demand Sincere Intentions

Non-local elements pertaining to Human Healing:

Placebo Effect, Quantum Healing, Meditation, Visualization, Energy Healing, the Mind-Body Connection, Epigenetics, Neuroplasticity, Coherence, Ancient Wisdom, the Chakra System

Non-local elements pertaining to the Physical World:

Energy, Frequencies, the Quantum Field, Wave-Particle Duality, Superposition, Quantum Entanglement, Tunneling, Morphic Fields, Electromagnetic Radiation, Electromagnetic Fields, Theory of Relativity, Quanta, the Hologram Hypothesis, Color is a Manifestation of Perception

Non-local elements pertaining to the World of the Infinite:

Divine Intelligence, the Quantum Field, God, Prayer, Meditation, the Art of Manifestation, Spirituality, Casual Potency of Consciousness, Non-local inputs, the Crown Chakra, Unity Consciousness, Bliss Consciousness, the Field of Uncertainty, the Field of Limitless Possibilities, Consciousness Field, the Hologram Hypothesis

Fields of Study – The Science:

Neuroscience, Biology, Physics, Physiology, Epigenetics, Psychology, Cosmology, Quantum Mechanics, Psychoneuroimmunology, Stellar Nucleosynthesis, Evolution, Cognition-Based Evolution, Quantum Information Science, Quantum Biology, Noetic Science, Plant Neurobiology

How I See It

It is clear enough that the science behind manifestation resides in the study of the non-local world. This is not surprising to me. What is remarkable however, is the trend in current research to explore and find answers pertaining to the non local realm.

I feel very fortunate to be alive during this extraordinary age of technology, innovation, and theoretical physics. Over my lifetime, I have witnessed the amazing advancements that have changed the way we live our daily lives.

I am looking forward to what today's innovative minds might propose in the realm of theoretical science tomorrow. I am anticipating an expanded knowledge base as new theories become proven theories. I hope exploration into the non-local world and the still mysterious aspects of quantum physics, will force impactful paradigm shifts as new discoveries get us closer to understanding the secrets of our existence.

A note from the Author: I'll Meet You There

"Out beyond ideas of wrongdoing and rightdoing there is a field. I'll meet you there." - Rumi

Dear Friend,

I admire you for reading this book. It shows your investment in personal growth and your determination to explore yourself and the universe you live in. Not everyone has the courage or the curiosity to embark on this journey of self-discovery, and I applaud you for taking the first step.

In a world filled with distractions and busy schedules, your commitment to self-improvement through knowledge is admirable. I am grateful for your dedication and I hope that this book has been able to provide you with insights and inspiration.

I have shared with you a vast amount of information, gathered through extensive research and my own personal experiences. My intention was to present it to you in a logical and organized manner, backed up by science and supporting evidence and data.

I hope that you have found this information useful and that it has shed light on the power you hold within yourself.

There is no one-size-fits-all approach to manifestation. Each individual is unique, and what resonates with one person may not resonate with another. Always trust your gut and take what works for you.

It's up to you to discover through trial and error the manifestation techniques that work for you. Use the activities and journal prompts I've given you as a guide, and make daily practice of mindfulness a priority. By doing so, you can harness the power within you and change your life for the better.

Don't forget the game changer that is gratitude. Each morning, wake up and identify at least three things you are grateful for. Make this a habit, and watch how it transforms your perspective and attracts positive experiences into your life.

I'm already working on my next book because there is so much more information I want to share with my readers. Science is constantly evolving, and even as I write this book, new research and theories are emerging in the quest to unravel the mysteries of life.

If you truly want to understand who you are and how you fit into the amazing universe we live in, it is essential to keep learning and expanding your knowledge. Be open to new ideas and discoveries, as they may hold the key to unlocking the hidden truths we all wish to discover.

Above all, I encourage you to seek for your truth, set intentions aligned with your deepest desires, and discover your life's purpose. You have unique gifts and talents that are surely connected to your purpose. You are the master of your own destiny.

To stay connected and increase your understanding, I invite you to join my online community. In this community, you will find like-minded women who are also on a journey of self-discovery and growth. In this supportive environment, we can share insights, evolve our understanding, empower each other, and elevate our individual paths to success and fulfillment.

Finally, I want you to know that you are important to me. I value each and every one of you as readers and learners. I would love to hear from you and continue this journey together. Please feel free to connect with me on my social media platforms or shoot me an email. My contact information is listed below.

As I continue my quest to understand our universe and the mysteries that surround it, I promise to never stop seeking for truth. If I get it right, I am humbled. If I get it wrong, equally humbled. Out beyond Rumi's field, I promise *to meet you there.*

Dream big. Believe. For you have nothing to lose and everything to gain. Remember, the power lies within you. Thank you once again for being a dedicated seeker and for allowing me to be a part of your journey.

With heartfelt appreciation,

Kristina Perdue

info@freakflagfun.com

Visit my website for more information on a WOMEN EMPOWERING WOMEN platform that I am currently developing. It promises to be a unique combination of courses for personal growth and manifestation along with a social network of support to connect you with like minded women around the world, ready to support you, challenge you, connect with you, hear your ideas, cheer you on, and ultimately make us all better people living lives of abundance and inspiring others to do the same!

https://www.freakflagfun.com

Made in the USA
Columbia, SC
15 February 2024

31596114R00167